A Winter in Majorca

edicions CORT

Can Troncoso street, 3-1r
Tel. 971 71 27 80
Fax 971 72 00 36
07001 Palma de Mallorca - Illes Balears
E-mail: comercial@edicionscort.com

Cover photo:
  Portrait by Auguste Charpentier
Back cover photo:
  Joan Tur

ISBN: 84-7535-414-9
Dipòsit legal: PM 953-1998

Printed by Impremta Politècnica

GEORGE SAND

A Winter in Majorca

Palma, Illes Balears
MCMXCVIII

Foreword

T HE eighth of November 1838. A boat docks in the port of Palma. A somewhat indifferent Majorca, receives another small group of travellers: a pale, slender, aristocratic looking young man of twenty-eight with a sickly air about him; a tall, vibrant brunette, in the prime of life, contemplates the marvellous view of the city, white, behind ramparts where summer still reigns; and finally two children, followed by a maid. They are M. Frederick Chopin, pianist and composer, and Madame Aurore Dupin, Baroness Dudevant, a writer known under the name of George Sand, accompanied by her two children.

All had gone smoothly until they arrived in Palma. They had made a short stop in Barcelona, where the weather had been perfect, and where they had enjoyed the city and its environments, showering it with praise. The crossing from Barcelona to Palma had taken place on a tranquil night, with the boat slipping through perfectly calm seas. Our passengers had even spent part of the night on the bridge, listening to the songs of the helmsman.

But it is in Majorca that things start to go wrong. Nothing works out. It is impossible to find comfortable lodgings, no decent piano is available, and the heating systems are most inadequate. People are hostile, doctors incompetent and the apothecaries know only few of the curative plants... Everything clouds over, including the weather, for, after an Indian summer, typical of Mediterranean countries at the end of October and early November, it becomes cold and humid, it begins to rain, but, above of all, the winds start blowing.

They start moving: from Palma they go to Establiments, and then on to Valldemossa. Finally, after a ninety day sojourn in Majorca, they flee. On their arrival in Barcelona, M. Chopin is so ill that all fear for his life; Mme. Sand is so angry and indignant that she swears to *'write with rancour'* about that terrible winter. And she does it with a vengeance, for Mme. Sand was bitterly resentful. Barely a year after that disastrous Majorcan adventure, that journey which she was to qualify as a complete fiasco, she started writing, in instalments, for the 'Revue des Deux Mondes'. These chapters would later be published in the form of a book titled *'A Winter in Majorca'*.

Why did they decide to travel to Majorca? What were they looking for? What did they know of the island? Why did the journey turn out to be a total failure?

They had met some months previously in Paris and fallen in love. M. Chopin was himself in a delicate situation: he had just broken his engagement with his fiancée, an engagement more or less imposed upon him by family and by circumstance. He was not in very good health. According to Heinrich Heine, he possessed a superhuman sensitivity; he guarded his private life ferociously; he shocked his friends and admirers with his changing moods, at one moment extremely charming, and a minute later, without any apparent reason, inexplicable outbursts, extravagant, violent... She was no great beauty, but extremely attractive: chestnut-coloured hair, gentle, serene eyes, a tender smile, a soft voice which she seldom raised for she preferred listening to speaking. Both were already famous. The mysterious and melancholic air of the musician, his bearing at the piano as he played, had conquered all women; his compositions had opened doors in Paris, in the Arts, in Literature and with the aristocracy.

Mme. Sand was considered a liberal woman, cultured, an excellent writer with clear and precise ideas on the social and political life of her times. She was already a celebrity. He was shy, somewhat untamed, and violently defended his private life. She led a life which was considered in conservative circles as *'wild and unruly'*: she had had several lovers, even before separating from her husband, she had had some scandalous love affairs; but, although she was judged as immoral and degenerate, all Mme. Sand wanted to do was to defend the right of women to love freely, without prejudice, without bitterness, without hypocrisy, a right that was presently tolerated only for men by the society of her times. She was capable of a tender and generous love, and always remained faithful to the end. At this moment, Mme. Sand's feelings and actions were consumed by emotion and passion.

They became friends, then lovers. Later, M. Chopin and Mme. Sand, decided to journey to Majorca. Doctors had recommended that Maurice, her eldest son who suffered from rheumatism, needed the sun of Spain to help him recuperate; on the other hand, M. Chopin, who suffered from frequent 'colds which degenerated into bronchitis' (no doctor had as yet diagnosed this illness, which was to terminate his life at the age of thirty-eight), would also benefit from a warmer climate. Their friends could not believe that they were going. She had travelled extensively, always curious to see new things, to sample new experiences, but would he be capable of living so far from his beloved Paris, his beloved piano and his beloved routine? And, on the other hand, were they not too different from one another? How long could a relationship between two such celebrities last? Mme. d'Agoult, a friend of theirs, writes: *"Knowing them, I am sure that within a month of being together, they will not be able to stand the sight of one another."* But a few days later she had to add: *"Reality is more beautiful than fiction (...) and George has fled with Chopin to fulfil their perfect love under the shadows of the myrtles in Palma"*.

Spiritual daughter of Rousseau, romantic and enthusiastic, Mme. Sand wanted to find more than the myrtles of Palma: she wanted the charm of an exotic landscape, undefiled nature, Moorish ruins, relics from the dark times of the Inquisition, knights, gypsies - that is to say, all the standard clichés of Spain magnified perhaps by the romanticism of the era. Without doubt, the Spanish intellectuals received her with the same admiration, the same welcome and the same eulogies as did the Parisians. As far as the peasants were concerned, she, as a true follower of Rousseau, imagined them to be pure and naive, those good, gentle and friendly savages. An Africa a little closer to France! One cannot blame her for this, everyone thought that way. A week after their arrival, M. Chopin wrote to his friend Fontana: *"I am in Palma, in the shade of palm-trees, cedars, aloes, orange-trees, lemon-trees, fig-trees and pomegranates. A turquoise sky, a sea of lapis-lazuli and emerald mountains. The air? The air is that of the sky. The days are sunny, all are dressed in summer clothing, it is hot; in the evenings one hears the sound of singing and guitars for hours. Enormous balconies, dating back to the Arabs, on which the vine-leaves fall. The city, like the rest of the country, is reminiscent of Africa. Briefly: a delicious life."*

Life, a honeymoon! But honeymoons do not last long, and theirs soon ends. M. Chopin falls ill. Most probably the doctors of Palma are not as good as those of Paris, but they certainly are less diplomatic. After examining him - an examination that would be cruelly ridiculed in letters and publications by both M. Chopin and Mme. Sand -, the Majorcan doctors come to the conclusion that he is a consumptive, that he should take his illness seriously, and that his condition is grave and contagious. Of course, they both do not believe a word of what they hear. He, because few can accept the idea that they are terminally ill. She, because she has no trust in the incompetent doctors of a delightful, but primitive, country. Had not the best doctors in Paris told her that her beloved was suffering from a nervous disorder that would disappear by the time he was forty? (In one way they were correct, for the musician died before his fortieth year.) On the other hand, how could she believe that it was better for them to leave. Was the Majorcan climate not good enough for him? Did not the French doctors insist that the Balearic sun would mend M. Chopin's bronchitis?

But M. Chopin was unable to cure his bronchitis, and this fact brought them face to face with reality.

People feared tuberculosis like the plague. No one would lodge them, serve them, or even approach them. There were no hotels in Palma, and if there had been, it is most likely they would have been refused shelter. The owner of the house they had rented in Establiments, fearful of the consequences of M. Chopin's illness, had forced them to leave.

They eventually found accommodation in the Charterhouse of Valldemossa, where the villagers apparently conspired to make life very difficult for them. All their misfortunes are well described in this very book. Can we trust her? Is it the complete truth that she has committed to paper?

Yes, most probably, but...

But Mme. Sand showed no curiosity whatsoever in discovering the actual status quo of the country they were going to visit. Spain was in the throes of a war, the War of Succession. Mme. Sand barely refers to it, and when she does, she speaks of 'bandits' as though she was referring to some notorious highwaymen. There were no battles in the streets of Palma, but the island was in a state of siege. The economy was suffering, and the isolation of Majorca was even more evident. People were very distrustful, particularly the country folk. Only a relatively short time had passed since the 'French War', the Napoleonic invasion. It is perfectly comprehensible that people were somewhat suspicious of a French woman who dressed as a man, who smoked, who lived with a man who was not her husband, and on top of it all, whose children accompanied her under such brazen circumstances.

A closed, puritanical society, full of prejudice reigned at that time in Majorca. Mme. Sand had hard words to describe the Majorcan high society, the way they lived, from what they lived, what their customs were. Perhaps with one or two exceptions, she probably never got to know the houses she describes. She was not admitted into this society, even though she promenaded through streets of Palma on the arm of the French Consul. Those who had had the opportunity of reading *'Lélia'* expected to meet a typically French woman, more elegant, more well-dressed, more like the French they had already met. Rumours of her scandalous love affairs had already reached Majorca. Mme. Sand was a great disenchantment.

But, if her criticism of upperclasses and the bourgeoisie was harsh, her censure of the peasants was pitiless. According to her, they were lazy, superstitious, ignorant, thieving and wicked... Their method of cultivating the earth was absurd, they had no idea of how to make agriculture profitable, they scorned all progress, they did not want to hear a word about industry... Poor things. *"They only know how to pray".* Was it perhaps, apart from the present political situation, that the peasants had no ambitions? *"They could inundate France with exquisite fruits".* Without doubt, but at that moment it was unnecessary, they had all they required and were not interested in big business. *"They treat pigs better than they treat people".* Ah, the episode of the pigs! Mme. Sand will never forget the return journey to Barcelona on a boat loaded with filthy, odorous hogs who did nothing but grunt the whole time.

And what of the food? No normal person could eat in Majorca, *"unless they liked lard and rancid olive-oil".* This does not take into account garlic. The smell of garlic permeated everything. Women had no charm whatsoever and reeked of garlic. Let us try to be a little understanding: it has not yet been scientifically proven that garlic is an aid in the prevention of coronary illnesses and that olive oil is healthier than any animal fat. Regarding lard, French peasants also consume this. Mme.

Sand must have known only a kitchen based on butter.

No, Mme. Sand was not impartial when she spoke of the Majorcans. *'A Winter in Majorca'* is not one of her best works and does not compare with any of her other literary achievements. It is a work written with hate and resentment. It is the fruit of a great disappointment. We know that Mme. Sand was a pleasant woman, well brought up and amiable. It was not like her to be so vulgar in her judgement and criticism, nor to indulge in such coarse cynicism instead of fine irony. It is not normal that a person, usually so sensitive to the problems of humanity, with elevated ideas on the freedom of the people and the rights of the underprivileged, should speak with such blatant cruelty about the people she got to know in Majorca. Yet, if there was no other way of handling the stupidity of these insensitive, cruel and badly educated people with whom she had had the bad luck of coming into contact, surely we have the right to believe that she, so cultured and sensitive, should have been more humane and understanding.

It is interesting to compare her observations with those of another traveller who visited Majorca at about the same time. M. Charles Dembowski, author of a book of notes and observations, titled *'Two Years in Spain and Portugal during the Civil War'* (he is referring to the War of Succession). He tells a story of the Chopin-Sand family in Valldemossa. M. Dembowski visited the village on the feast-day of Saint Anthony, where he saw the benediction of the animals and participated in the fiesta. Half-way through the celebrations, he left in order to deliver post to the foreigners in the Charterhouse. On his return, he found the mayor and the parish priest most annoyed by the lack of interest shown by *"those people"* towards the customs and celebrations of their village. *"Do you realize,"* said the priest, *"that this must be a very strange French woman indeed. She speaks to no one, never leaves the monastery and has never appeared in Church, not even on Sundays. How many mortal sins she must be amassing, God only knows. Furthermore, the apothecary, who also lives in the Charterhouse, has told me that she makes her own cigarettes, drinks coffee at all hours, sleeps during the day and spends the night writing and smoking. I beg of you, dear sir, since you know her, to tell us what has this woman come to do in Majorca in the middle of winter?"*

It is also interesting to note that while Mme. Sand asserts that there is no one less hospitable than the Majorcan, M. Dembowski writes in the same chapter: *"Of my journey to the interior of the island (...) I retain a growing feeling of goodwill towards the hospitable people who inhabit that land; not all villages had an inn, and in order not to spend the night in the open, one was forced to ask for accommodation from the people. They were happy to welcome you, gave you their best bed, gave you a place beside the kitchen chimney, and allowed you to share in the preparation of the meal. The following day the host would thank you for having chosen his home, and normally refused any financial recompensation".*

Is Mme. Sand therefore lying? Certainly not. She just had bad luck and she had met only disagreeable people. Without doubt she is exaggerating, especially when she repeats things that have been said of her, for she most probably had not understood a word of what had been said to her in Mallorquin. But, above all, instead of spending a holiday with her lover, she found herself nursing an invalid. She mocked the criticisms of her walks through the cemetery by moonlight, the fact that she smoked, that she dressed as a man, and that she never set foot in Church. Perhaps she should have been more discreet, in the same way as when she visited her home village, where customs were less free than those of Paris. But that people were so cruel with poor M. Chopin and his bronchitis, that they told him to his face that he was dying, that they denied him lodging and refused to sell him food, (she had had to resort to the French Consul to solve their food problem), this was something that Mme. Sand could not forgive.

On the other hand, M. Chopin ended up loathing Majorca.

That is quite obvious. How could someone suffering from tuberculosis live on such a humid island? At that time tuberculosis was totally unknown. He must have also been very disillusioned by this adventure. Not only did he feel ill, but instead of a delightful journey with his beloved, it was a nightmare shared with a nurse. Both of them, but above all him, if we are to believe Mme. Sand, had only one thought in mind, and that was to leave Majorca and Spain as soon as possible. On top of it all, they did not find happiness until they returned to Paris; for the doctors had recommended that M. Chopin should remain in the South of France until the Spring, and so they settled in Marseilles. If this serves as some consolation to the Majorcans, it is said the people of Marseilles also annoyed Mme. Sand. Not so at the beginning: in a letter written to her friend, Carlotta Marliani, on the 26th of February, just after their arrival in Marseilles, Mme. Sand writes, *"I bring you news of our invalid, for you are as interested in his state of health as I am. He is better, much better. He no longer spits blood, he sleeps, he coughs less. And, above all, he is in France! He can sleep in a comfortable bed that won't be burned the next day. People do not recoil from him when he extends his hand. We are caring well for him and he has access to all that medicine has to offer."* But a month later, she tells her friend, *"There is an uproar at our house-door. The literary mob is after me and the musical riffraff is after Chopin. To protect him, I told them he was dead. If this continues, I will send out our death notices, so that they can finally weep and leave us in peace."*

Nevertheless, it would be an error to believe that during those terrible three months spent in Majorca, Mme. Sand and M. Chopin did nothing else but upset the locals and be extremely unhappy. Mme. Sand wrote a lot, in spite of, as she herself said, *"having to cope with everything"*: she kept house, she cooked, she gave lessons to the children, she tended to all family problems. She corrected her novel *'Lélia'*, and, above all, she produced the first draft of what was to become one of her most important works: *"Spiridion"*. The monasteries which she had visited in Barcelona and Majorca furnished the background. The evolution of her social and religious ideas, the influence of her friend Leroux, the theories of Lamennais were the springboard for her story. The truth was that she had to write because she was in need of money. Those peasants who profited from this bizarre group of people, these heretics in a permanent state of mortal sin, were unaware that they were not as rich as they appeared to be. Both Mme. Sand and M. Chopin lived off their work. Because of the Civil War, Majorca was in a state of siege and so their money did not arrive that easily.

M. Chopin, regardless of his illness, also produced a tremendous amount of work. Opinions vary as to what he composed or corrected during his Majorcan stay, but it is certain that he composed the Second Ballad - Opus 38, in F, the Scherzo Nº3 - Opus 39, in C sharp minor, the Mazurka - Opus 67 in A minor and the Preludes, the most famous of which is the Prelude, Nº15 - in D flat, commonly known as "The Raindrops".

A legend has replaced reality regarding the circumstances of the creation of these works. The first comes to us through Mme. Sand's autobiography, *"The Story of my Life"*, written long after her Majorcan adventure, and which, according to her biographer, André Maurois, is *"the most romantic of all her novels"*. Probably these momentous reminiscences became more fantastic with time, and her romantic spirit only added to it. It appears that all the work M. Chopin composed in Majorca, was produced while in a state of ailing, apprehensive and melancholic exaltation, surrounded by terrifying and fantasmagorical visions. The cell which he occupied in the Charterhouse, as he himself describes in a letter to a friend, was a "coffin", the turbulent weather, the wind, the rain, all added to create a romantic setting, and history gave it a greater and more grandiose dimension. The well known words that the writer Oscar Wilde puts into the mouth of a character in his book *"The Portrait of Dorian Gray"*:

"What a charming piece you are playing! I ask myself if Chopin did not write it in Majorca, with the sea roaring about his house, splashing the window panes with salt water ..." exemplifies the background into which the 'Majorcan' compositions were placed, and which distanced them more and more from reality.

As a matter of fact, most critics concur that the Majorcan compositions of M. Chopin appear to have been created with remarkable balance and serenity, reflecting a greater interior peace than in many others. The Prelude, N°15 - in D flat, "The Raindrops", does not seem to have been 'improvised' on a day of furious storms and rain, on the contrary, it shows a great capacity for harmony and a superb control of composition.

As for the book *'A Winter in Majorca'*, on the day of its publication in Majorca it evoked angry and passionate protests. How dared George Sand write such things, how could she spread such slander? How could she call Majorca 'the island of monkeys'? How dared she generalise and say what she said, she who only knew a small part of Majorca and only a few Majorcans? Mme. Sand was delighted at the indignation she had caused. How could she possibly be affected by the anger of a people she so despised?

Decidedly, Mme. Sand and the Majorcans did not understand one another. Yet, in her book, *'A Winter in Majorca'*, George Sand, a writer who usually gave greater importance to analysing feelings than to background, some of the most beautiful and ardent descriptions of nature are to be found. Each phrase, each sentence describing the landscape, the mountains, the sea, are the most beautiful that have ever been written about Majorca. It is not worth repeating them here: one should read them in the order in which they were written. *"Everything is so lovely, that at moments I have the impression that I will bore my reader with my adjectives"*, she said. No, she does not bore us, she perhaps makes us see things with different eyes, she gives us a different perspective. What a shame that she came to Majorca loaded with prejudices, ignorant of its past, and refusing to recognize its reality. What a shame that M. Chopin was ill and cold, and that their journey did not turn out the way they had imagined it.

It is amusing that this book, so forgotten, never cited in literary anthologies, judged as one of her minor works, is edited and re-edited precisely here in Majorca, and is almost the only work of hers known to the Majorcans. What would she have had to say about that?...

Palma, 30th Octuber, 1997

MARIA FCA. VIDAL

A Winter in
Majorca

George Sand a drawing by Augustus Charpentier.

Author's note

T HE date of this book will be found in a letter dedicated to my friend François Rollinat. The reflections which open Chapter IV justify the book, and I can do no better than refer to them here: 'Why travel, unless you must?' Today, returning from the same latitude but crossed at a different point in Southern Europe, I once more repeat, as I did after my visit to Majorca: 'It is not so much a question of travelling as of getting away; which of us has not some pain to dull, or some yoke to cast off?'

Nohant, August 25th, 1855.

GEORGE SAND

Letter from a former traveller to a friend who stayed at home

HOME-BOUND as you are, my dear François, you believe that, carried away by the proud and unruly hobby-horse of my independence, I have known no greater pleasure in this world than that of crossing seas and mountains, lakes and valleys. Alas! My sweetest, most beautiful journeys have been made at my own fireside, with my feet on the warm hearth and my elbows resting on the frayed arms of my grandmother's armchair. Doubtless you will have done the same, equally pleasant and a thousand times more poetic: which is why I suggest that you do not regret too much having missed sweating under a tropical sun, freezing your feet on snow-bound Polar wastes, braving frightful storms at sea, beating off attacks by bandits, and similar ordeals and hardships which you encounter in your imagination every evening, without so much as removing your slippers, and with no more serious damage than a few cigar burns in the lining of your smoking jacket.

In order to reconcile you to having been deprived of actual physical movement in wide open spaces, I am sending an account of my last journey outside France, in the certainty that I shall arouse your compassion rather than your envy, and that you will conclude that too high a price can be paid for some outbursts of admiration and one or two hours of hard-won delight wrested from ill-fortune. This account, written a year ago, has now earned me a most fulminating and laughable tirade of abuse from the natives of Majorca themselves. It is a pity that it is too long to be published as a sequel to my story, for the tone in which it is conceived and the grace of the reproaches addressed to me would bear out my view of the hospitality and delicacy with which the Majorcans welcome foreigners. It would be an interesting and justificatory document; but who would venture to read it through to the end? Besides, since if it is considered conceited and vain to disclose the compliments one receives, would it not be even more absurd and foolish, in these modern times, to make a fuss of the abuse of which one is the object?

I therefore refrain from bothering you with these pages and confine myself to tell you, as a final comment on these guileless people of Majorca, that after having read my account, forty of the most skilful lawyers of Palma met to draw up a terrible indictment against the 'immoral writer' who had taken the liberty of deriding their love of profit and their painstaking dedication to the breeding of pigs. As the 'other one' has said, the whole forty felt and thought as four.

But let us leave in peace these good people who were so enraged against me. They have had time to calm down, and I to overlook their way of behaving, talking and writing. Among the inhabitants of that beautiful island, I now only recall five or six people whose kindly welcome and friendly attitude will always remain in my memory as a compensation and a blessing for the hardness of my lot. If I have not mentioned them by name, it is because I do not consider myself as sufficiently important to render them famous by my gratitude; but I am certain (and I think I have stressed this in the course of my narrative) that they too will have a friendly enough memory of me not to believe themselves included in my disrespectful mockeries, nor to doubt the sincerity of my feelings for them.

I have said nothing to you about Barcelona where, nevertheless, we spent several busy days before embarking for Majorca. To go by sea from Port-Vendres to Barcelona in a good steamer and during fine weather is a delightful trip. In the month of November, on the shores of Catalonia, we rediscovered the spring-like air we had just been breathing at Nîmes but which had deserted us in Perpignan; and summer heat awaited us in Majorca. At Barcelona a fresh sea breeze tempered the heat of the sun, and swept every cloud away from a vast horizon framed by distant mountain peaks, some black and bare, others white with snow. We made a short excursion into the countryside; the robust little Andalusian horses which bore us needed a good meal of oats first if they were to return us swiftly back under the walls of the citadel should we come up against any predicament.

You well know that in 1838 the factionists formed guerrilla bands and overran the whole region, blocking roads, invading towns and villages, holding even the humblest dwelling-places to ransom, seizing villas as close as half a league from the town, and storming out unexpectedly from every rock shelter to assault the traveller for their money or their lives.

Nonetheless, we ventured for several leagues along the coast and met only some detachments of Queen Christina's partisans on their way to Barcelona. They had been described as the finest troops of Spain; indeed they were men of fine presence and not too badly equipped considering they had just been on campaign. But both men and horses were so thin, the former with yellow wan faces and the latter with such hanging heads and gaunt sides, that the very sight of them made one feel hungry.

A still more depressing sight was that of the fortifications cast around the most humble of settlements. Before the door of each poor cottage stood a modest rampart of dry stone, and a castellated tower as thick as a piece of nougat; the loopholed walls around each roof showed clearly that the inhabitants in these fertile fields did not feel in the least bit secure. In many places these miserable little defences bore recent traces of attack.

Once through the formidable and mighty fortifications of Barcelona, with a perplexing number of gates, draw-bridges, posterns and ramparts, we found nothing further to suggest the city was at war. Behind a triple ring of cannons, and isolated from the rest of Spain by banditry and civil war, the scintillating youth of Barcelona sunned itself on the *rambla,* a long avenue lined with trees and buildings similar to our boulevards: the women, beautiful, graceful and coquettish, concerned solely with the folds of their mantillas and the play of their fans; the men busy with their cigars, laughing, chatting, ogling the ladies, discussing the Italian opera, apparently not interested in what might be happening beyond the city walls. But once night had come, when the opera was over and the guitars fallen silent, and the city was given over to the roaming of the vigilant night-watchmen, the only sounds to be heard, above the monotonous surging of the sea, were the sentries' sinister challenges and still more sinister shots. These shots rang out in irregular intervals, now singly, now in rapid volleys, from places near and far, sometimes independently, sometimes in reply, but continuing until the first light of dawn. Then for an hour or two all was silent, and the well-to-do seemed to sleep soundly, while the port came to life and the seafolk began to stir.

If, during the carefree hours of gossip and fun, you ventured to ask what those strange and frightening night noises had meant, the smiling reply would be that they were nobody's concern, and that it would be unwise to enquire further.

Part One

Frederick Chopin engraving made in Leipzig.

Chapter 1

According to an inscription carved on a rock at the entrance of the Mer-de-Glace, it must have been about fifty years ago that two English tourists discovered the valley of Chamonix.

The claim is a rather bold one if one takes into account the geographical position of this valley, but to a certain extent a fair one if these two tourists, whose names I can't remember, were indeed the first to draw the attention of poets and painters to the romantic landscapes where Byron conceived his wonderful *Manfred*.

In general, it may be said that Switzerland was not discovered by fashionable society or by artists until the last century. Jean-Jaques Rousseau is the true Christopher Columbus of Alpine poetry and, as so well observed by M. de Chateaubriand, he is also the father of romanticism in our language.

I am unable to advance quite the same claims to immortality as Jean-Jacques, but when searching for something akin, I find that I might have made myself as famous as the two Englishmen in the valley of Chamonix, had I claimed the honour of having discovered Majorca. But the world has become so exacting that it would not be enough for me to have chiselled my name on some Balearic rock: a relatively accurate description would have been demanded of me, or at the very least a fairly poetical account of my travels that would tempt tourists to make the journey. But since I felt far from enchanted on that island, I renounced the glory of my discovery, recording it neither on rock nor on paper.

Had I written under the strain of the worries and frustrations which I suffered at that time, it would have been impossible for me to boast about this discovery, and every one of my readers would have commented that it could not be as bad as made out to be; and yet there was certainly something to write about, for Majorca is, especially for painters, one of the most beautiful and least known places on earth. There, where it is only possible to describe the picturesque beauty, literary expression is so poor and inadequate that I never dreamt of attempting it. It takes the artist's pencil and the engraver's burin to reveal the grandeur and splendour of Nature to lovers of foreign travel.

Today, these long dormant memories were aroused by a beautiful book which I found on my table, the other morning, entitled, *Souvenirs d'un Voyage d'Art à l'île de Majorque* (Records of an Artist's Journey to the Island of Majorca), by J.-B Laurens.

It was a real joy to rediscover Majorca with its palm trees, its aloes, its Arab monuments and Grecian costumes. I recognized all the poetically-coloured scenes, and relived all the impressions which I thought I had long forgotten. Not a single hut or clump of bushes failed to arouse in me a world of memories, as they say nowadays; and then I felt, that if not capable of describing my own journey, I was at least able to review that of M. Laurens. He is an intelligent and painstaking artist, a swift and conscientious worker, and to whom the honour should be awarded, which I had attributed to myself, of having discovered the Island of Majorca.

The journey of M. Laurens to the heart of the Mediterranean, to shores where the sea is at times as inhospitable as their inhabitants, is much more commendable than the excursion of our two Englishmen to Montavert. Nevertheless, if Europe ever became sufficiently civilized to do away with customs officers and police, those outward manifestations of international mistrust and dislike, and if a direct steamer service were to link France to those domains, Majorca would soon prove to be an overwhelming rival to Switzerland. The trip could be made in a few days, and travellers would certainly find delicate beauties and strange and sublime splendours - a new sustenance for painters.

At the moment I cannot conscientiously recommend this trip except to those artists of robust physique and ardent spirits. No doubt the day will come when frail amateurs, and even lovely women, will be able to visit Palma with no more exhaustion and inconvenience than going to Geneva.

M. Laurens worked for some years as illustrator for M. Taylor's survey of the ancient monuments of France. Last year, left to his own devices, he decided to visit the Balearic Islands. He had so little information about them that he confesses it was with a beating heart he stepped ashore there, fearing many disappointments to his golden dreams. But what he had gone to look for, he was to find and he was to realise all his hopes - because, let me repeat, Majorca is the painter's Eldorado. Everything there is picturesque, from the peasant's hut which has preserved minor details of design in the traditional Arab style, to the ragged urchin glorying in his 'imposing uncleanness', as Heinrich Heine says of the Veronese herbsellers. The character of the landscape, richer in vegetation than the African countryside, does not yield to it in spaciousness and is more simple and calm. It is a green Switzerland beneath a Calabrian sky, with the silence and solemnity of the Orient.

In Switzerland streams rush everywhere accompanied by the incessant activity of clouds. This results in a constant changing of colours and a continuity of movement that cannot be successfully caught on a painter's canvas. Nature seems to be teasing the artist. But in Majorca she awaits and welcomes him. There, the vegetation is lofty and strange but has none of the lavishness that often blurs the outlines of a Swiss landscape. Rocky peaks stand silhouetted against a sparkling sky, the palm tree leans over the precipice without the wind disturbing its magnificent chevelure, and everything, down to the stunted cactus by the roadside, seems to be posing with a kind of vanity to delight the eye.

First of all, allow me to give a concise description of the largest Balearic island, using the style of an article in a geographic dictionary. This is by no means as simple as one may suppose, especially when one is compelled to collect the necessary data on the spot. Spanish caution and insular distrust forbids a foreigner to ask even the most insignificant geographical question, unless he wants to run the risk of being taken for a political agent. The good M. Laurens, who dared sketch a ruined tower which caught his eye, was arrested by the Constable on a charge of making a plan of the fortress.[1] Thereafter our traveller, determined to fill his sketch-book elsewhere than in the State prisons of Majorca, limited his enquiries to mountain paths and to documentary research into ruins. After having spent four months in Majorca I should have found out no more than he, had I not availed myself of what little information happened to have been published. But once again my doubts arose; the authors of the works - which are, in any case, out of date - contradict and

---

[1] 'The only object that caught my attention on this coast was a dark, ochre-coloured ruin, surrounded by a cactus hedge. It was the Castle of Sóller. I had hardly drawn the outlines of my sketch when four individuals, with such fearsome expressions on their faces that made me want to laugh, swooped upon me. I was guilty of making, contrary to the laws of the kingdom, a plan of the fortress; and at once the fortress became my prison!

'My command of Spanish being too limited to explain the absurdity of their proceedings, I had to appeal for protection to the local French Consul in Sóller but, despite his intervention I was a prisoner for three hours, guarded by the Constable, Señor Sei-Dedos ('Six-Fingers'), a veritable Dragon of the Hesperides. At times I felt like hurling this comical dragon, military trappings and all, from the top of his tower into the sea, but each time the expression on his face disarmed my anger. Had I had Charlet's talent, I would have spent my time studying my Constable, for he was indeed a an excellent type to caricature. Besides, I forgave him his zeal on behalf of State security. Hitherto his only distraction had been smoking a cigar and gazing out at sea, so naturally he seized the opportunity I gave him of doing something different for a change.. I returned to Sóller, greatly amused at having been taken for an enemy of the fatherland and its constitution.'

insult one another so arrogantly, that I cannot avoid rectifying certain inaccuracies, though by doing so I may incur others. So here is my article, and to prove myself a true traveller, I shall at once declare its unquestionable superiority to all those that have preceded it.

Palma and the harbour about XIX century (J. B. Laurens, 1839).

Chapter II

MAJORCA, which M. Laurens, like the Romans, calls *Balearis Major,* and which, according to Dr. Juan Dameto, the king of Majorcan historians, was formerly known as *Clumba* or *Columba* - is now known as Mallorca, a corruption; and its capital has never been named 'Mallorca', as many of our geographers have made out, but Palma.

This island is the largest and most fertile of the Balearic Archipelago, remnant of a continent whose basin must have been flooded by the Mediterranean and which, without doubt, once joined Spain to North Africa, shares the climate and produce of both these regions. It lies 25 leagues south-west of Barcelona, 45 from the nearest point of the African coast and, I believe some 95 to 100 leagues from the port of Toulon. It covers a total area of 1,234 square miles[2] and has a circumference of 143 miles; the greatest length is 54 miles and the least, 28 miles. The population, which numbered 136,000 in 1787, is today about 160,000; during this same period, that of Palma has risen from 32,000 to 36,000.

The temperature varies considerably with the lie of the land. Summer is scorching hot in the plain; but the winter climate is

---

[2] 'Medida por el ayre. Cada milla de mil pasos geométricos y un paso de 5 pies geométricos' (Miguel de Vargas, *Descripciones de las islas de Pitiusas y Baleares.* Madrid, 1787)

greatly affected by the chain of mountains which stretches from north-east to south-west, (this direction suggesting its identity with the land masses of Africa and Spain, the nearest points of which have the same inclination and correspond to the same general pattern). Thus, Miguel de Vargas records that in Palma, on a January day during the terrible winter of 1784-5 the Réaumur thermometer only once registered 6 degrees above freezing point; on other days the temperature rose to 16, but the mean was 11. Now this temperature was more or less what we experienced in a normal winter in Valldemosa, which is reputed to be one of the coldest parts of the island. On the severest nights, with two inches of snow, the thermometer read 6 or 7 degrees. By eight o'clock in the morning it had risen to 9 or 10, and by midday to 12 or 14. Usually, around three o'clock, after the sun had disappeared from view behind the surrounding mountains, the thermometer sank suddenly to 9, or even 8, degrees.

The island is often swept by raging north winds, and in some years the winter rains fall with an abundance and continuity of which we in France have no conception. On the whole, on the southern parts which face Africa, the climate is healthy and flourishing, and are protected from furious boreal storms by the northern mountain chain and the mighty escarpment. Thus, the general plan of the island is an inclined plane sloping from north-west to south-east, and navigation, virtually impossible in the north on account of jagged projections and precipices which abound on this coastline, *'rugged and frightful, without shelter or refuge'* (Miguel de Vargas), is safe and easy in the south.

•   •   •

The ancients had good reason to call Majorca the 'Golden Isle'; for despite storms and other rigours, it is extremely fertile and its products are of excellent quality. The pure and fine wheat is exported to Barcelona where it is exclusively used to bake the white, light pastry called *pan de Mallorca*. The Majorcans import, for their own use, a coarser and cheaper wheat from Galicia and Biscay, with the result that, in a land where first-class wheat is plentiful, the bread is loathsome. I cannot say if this transaction is beneficial to them.

In our own central provinces, where agriculture is very backward, farming methods display only the peasants' obstinacy and ignorance. The same, but with greater truth, applies to Majorca, for although the land is farmed with meticulous care, agriculture is still in its infancy. Nowhere else have I seen the soil worked so patiently and so ineffectually. Even the simplest machinery is unknown: men's arms, very lean and puny compared with ours, do everything but to an incredibly slow tempo. Half a day is needed to till less land than would be tilled here in two hours, and five or six of the strongest men are needed to shift a load which one of our smallest porters would carry off cheerfully on his shoulders.

Despite this apathy, every inch of the land is cultivated, and as far as one can tell, well cultivated. These islanders are said never to have experienced famine; yet midst all the treasures of nature and beneath the finest skies, their lives are more rough and more frugal than those of our peasants.

Travellers repeatedly elaborate on the good fortune of the southerners, whose faces and picturesque costumes seem to reflect one long sunny Sunday, and whose mindlessness and lack of prevision they interpret as the epitome of pastoral tranquility. This is an error into which I myself have often fallen, but from which I am now safely delivered, especially since my visit to Majorca.

Nothing in the world is as dreary and morose as this poor peasant who knows no better than to pray, sing and work, and who never thinks. His prayer is an absurd formula which his spirit is unable to unravel; his physical work is an operation which he is unable to improve by any intellectual effort; and his song is the expression of that bleak melancholy which unknowingly overpowers him, leaving him totally unaware of its moving poetry. Were it not that vanity occasionally arouses him from his topor and sends him out to dance, his holidays would be devoted wholly to sleep.

But I have already gone beyond the limits I had set for myself. Strictly speaking, the geographical essay should handle, first of all, produce and commercial economy, and should deal only in the final paragraphs, after Cereals and Cattle, with Man.

In all the geographic reference books I have consulted, this brief notice appears under the heading *Baleares*. I corroborate it here, although certain details may have to be reconsidered later. *'These islanders are most amiable*, (We know that, in every island the human race falls into two categories: those who are cannibals and the 'most amiable'). *They are gentle and hospitable; rarely do they commit crimes, and theft is almost unknown among them.'* I shall certainly have to return to this text later on.

But first of all, let us discuss the produce; for I have heard that certain speeches (indiscreet to say the least) have been made in the Chamber of Deputies regarding a possible occupation of Majorca by the French; and I assume that should this book fall into the hands of one of our Deputies, he will be far more interested by the section on produce than by my philosophical reflections on the islanders' intellectual prowess.

• • •

So lets get back to my pigs. These animals, dear reader, are the most handsome on earth. With the most guileless admiration, Dr. Miguel de Vargas has given us a portrait of a young pig who, at the age of one and a half years, weighed in at twenty-four *arrobas*, that is to say some six hundred pounds. At that time, pig-farming for profit in Mallorca did not enjoy the reputation it has today. Trade in livestock was hampered by the greed of the financiers to whom the Spanish Government entrusted, that is to say sold, the victualling contracts. In virtue of their discretionary powers, these speculators opposed all livestock export while reserving the rights of unlimited import.

This usurious practice discouraged farmers from cattle breed-ing. Meat was fetching very low prices and with export being forbidden, they faced ruin, so they let their cattle die out. The extinction of the herds was rapid. The historian whom I quote sadly recalls the times of the Arab occupation, when the mountain of Artá alone grazed more head of fertile cows and noble bulls than could be found today on all the plains of Mallorca.

This was not the only way in which the natural riches of the country were being put to waste. The same writer recalls that the mountains, especially those of Torella and the Galatzo, were covered with the finest trees on earth. He mentions an olive which had a girth of forty-two feet, and a diameter of 14 feet; but these magnificent forests were ravaged by naval carpenters, who, at the time of the Spanish expedition against Algiers, constructed an entire flotilla of gunboats with them. The harassment to which the owners were afterwards subjected, and the miserly damages paid, induced the Majorcans to destroy their woodland resources instead of pursuing a policy of afforestation. Today, the vegetation is still so abundant and lovely that it does not occur to the traveller to regret the past; but now, as formally, in Majorca as throughout Spain, corruption rules. However, the traveller never hears a complaint, for, at the start of an unjust regime, fear keeps the oppressed silent, and once the harm has been done, silence continues from force of habit.

Although the tyranny of the contractors is at an end, Majorcan livestock has not recovered from its destruction, and is unlikely to do so while the export privileges are still restricted

The port of Palma with the Cathedral. (Pub. by J. Hetzel. Paris, 1856).

to trading in pigs. Very few cows and oxen are to be seen in the plain, and none at all in the mountains. Their meat is lean and tough. Though of a good breed, the sheep are badly fed and poorly cared for; the goats, being of African stock, do not render the tenth part of the milk that ours give.

The soil lacks nourishment, and in spite of the praise that the Majorcans bestow on their agricultural methods, I still consider that the seaweed which they use for manure is a very poor fertiliser, and that their fields do not produce what one would expect under so bountiful a sky. I have carefully examined the wheat, which is so precious that the inhabitants consider themselves unworthy of its consumption. It is identical to that which is grown in our central provinces, and which our peasants call white, or Spanish, wheat; and ours is equally good despite the difference in climate. However, the wheat of Majorca should have a marked superiority over that grown by us in the face of our harsh winters and unreliable springs. And yet our agricultural methods are crude and we have a lot to learn in this field; but the French farmer displays an energy and a perseverance which the Majorcan would scorn as rash.

Figs, olives, almonds and oranges grow in abundance in Majorca; yet, for the want of roads, trading is not as extensive as it could be. Five hundred oranges sell on the spot for about three francs; but to transport this cumbersome load on mule-back from the centre of the island to the coast would cost nearly as much again. On these grounds one can understand the neglect of orange cultivation in the centre of the island. These trees abound only in the valley of Sóller and in the vicinity of other coves, where our small ships can come and load. They could, no doubt, be successfully planted elsewhere: for instance, we had superb lemons and oranges on our mountain of Valldemosa, one of the coldest parts of the island, which ripened later than those of Sóller. We picked lemons as big as a man's head at La Granja, an estate in another mountainous region. It seems to me that the island of Majorca alone could keep the whole of France supplied with these exquisite fruits, at the same price as is paid for the detestable oranges we import from Hyères and the Genoese coast. This trade, which the Majorcans boast about so much, is therefore, like everything else, thwarted by their superb negligence.

The same thing could be said about the vast produce of the olive trees, certainly the finest in the world, which the Majorcans, thanks to their Moorish inheritance, cultivate perfectly. Unfortunately, they only know how to extract a rancid and nauseating oil which would appall us, and which they will never be able to export in quantity, except to Spain where a taste for this loathsome oil is equally prevalent. But Spain herself is rich in olive trees, and if Majorca provides her with oil, it must be at a very low price.

In France we consume large quantities of extravagantly priced olive oil of a very poor quality. If our refining methods were known in Majorca and if Majorca had a road network and, finally, if merchant shipping were organized to that particular end, we should have plenty of pure oil, regardless of the severity of the winter. I am well aware that the industrialists who cultivate the olive of peace in France will always prefer to sell a few tons of this precious liquid for its weight in gold, allowing our grocers to blend it into casks of peanut or colza oil to offer it to us at 'cost price'. Yet it would be strange if we obstinately continued to produce this commodity in our harsh climate, when only twenty-four sailing hours away we could obtain a cheaper and better oil.

However, our French monopolists need have no fear: though we promised the Majorcans - or even the Spaniards in general - to obtain our supplies from them and greatly increase their wealth, we would not be able to make them change their ways. They so profoundly disdain any improvements originating from abroad, and especially from France, that I doubt that any amount of money (which they do not, on the whole, despise) would impel them to deviate in the least from the traditions inherited from their forefathers[3].

---

[3] This oil is so offensive that every house, man and carriage on the island of Majorca, and even the very air of the fields, becomes impregnated with its stench. Since it is an integral part of their cooking, the fumes rise up two or three times a day from their homes and the walls are steeped in it. If, deep in the country, you loose your way, you need only sniff the air, and if a rancid scent wafts past your nostrils on the wings of a breeze, you may be sure to find a house hidden behind some rock or clump of cacti. If in the wildest and loneliest areas, this scent pursues you, look up and you will see some hundred paces away, a Majorcan on his donkey riding down the hill towards you. This is neither a joke nor an exaggeration, but the literal truth.

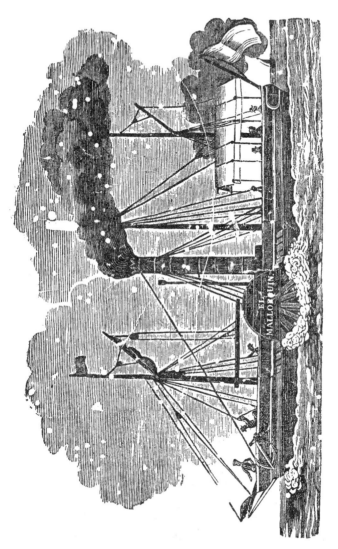

An old engraving from the Guasp Museum showing "El Mallorquín", (The Majorcan).

Chapter III

THE Majorcan, not knowing how to fatten cattle, being unable to make use of wool or milk cows (his dislike of milk and butter is as deep as his contempt of industry); or grow enough wheat to venture eating bread; barely bringing himself to cultivate the mulberry and gather silk; having lost the art of carpentry, which once flourished on the island and is now completely forgotten; possessing no horses (since Spain still lays a maternal hand on all Majorcan foals, and takes them into her armies, the pacific Majorcan is not so foolish as to maintain the cavalry of the kingdom at his own expense); nor deeming it necessary to provide a single negotiable road or path in the entire island (because the export rights were left to the whims of a government too busy to concern itself with such trivialities): vegetated, with nothing whatever to do except tell his beads and mend his breeches, more worn out than those of Don Quixote, his prototype in poverty and pride, - until the pig came along and saved the situation. A new era of prosperity began when its export was declared legal.

In centuries to come the Majorcans will call this the Age of the Pig - just as Moslems refer, in their history, to the Age of the Elephant.

Now, neither the olive nor the carob-bean lie neglected on the ground, the cactus-fig no longer serves a plaything for children, and mothers of families have learned to economize in beans and potatoes. The pig permits no waste, for the pig lets nothing be lost; it is the finest example of prodigal voracity, coupled with simplicity of tastes and habits, that can be offered to the world. Hence he came to enjoy in Mallorca rights and privileges which no one had so far dreamed of according to man. Dwellings have been enlarged and made airier; fruit, which used to rot on the ground, has now been gathered, sorted and stored; and steamships, once considered needless and unreasonable, now connect Majorca to the mainland.

It was therefore thanks to the pig that I visited the island of Majorca; had I thought of going three years before, the idea of such a long and hazardous journey in a small sailing ship would have made me abandon it. But, with the legalization of pig importation, civilisation has penetrated Majorca.

A beautiful little steamer was bought in England which, though not built to defy the terrible north winds which can rage here, in calm weather conveys two hundred pigs to Barcelona, and a few passengers as well.

It is quite touching to see with what tenderness these gentlemen (I am not referring to the passengers) are treated on board, and with what care they are put ashore. The captain of the steamer is a most agreeable man who, because of living and conversing with such noble beasts, has acquired their tone of voice and even some of their unselfconsciousness. If a passenger complains of the noise they make, the captain tells him that it is the sound of gold coins rolling on the counter. If a woman is squeamish enough to complain of the foul odour permeating the ship, her husband is there to tell her that money never smells and that, without pigs, she would have neither silk dresses, French hats nor Barcelonese mantillas. If anyone is sea-sick, he need expect no help from the crew; for pigs, too, are subject to seasickness which is accompanied by a splenetic languor and a readiness to lie down and die that must be combated at all costs. Therefore, foreswearing all compassion and sympathy in order to save the lives of his precious clients, the captain in person, armed with a whip, plunges into their midst, followed by the sailors and cabin-boys, each grabbing up what ever lies to hand, whether an iron bar or a piece of rope: in an instant the whole herd, which were lying motionless on their sides, are given a paternal thrashing, forced to rise and move around, and through violent exercise offset the disastrous influence of the ship's rolling and pitching.

On our return from Majorca to Barcelona, in the month of March, the heat was stifling, yet we were unable to set foot on deck. Even had we braved the danger of having our legs bitten by some bad-tempered pig, the captain would never have allowed us to upset them by our presence. They were quiet during the first hours of the journey; but, at about midnight, the pilot noticed that the animals were sleeping very dejectedly and were falling into, what appeared to be, a black depression. So the whip was applied; and regularly, every quarter of an hour, we were awakened by such frightful howls and shrieks on the one part from the beaten pigs, and on the other, the inspired encouragement of the captain to his men -that on several occasions we believed the herd was devouring the crew.

When the ship anchored, we longed for nothing more than to separate ourselves from such strange company, and I must admit that the islanders too were beginning to bore me as much as their charges; but we were only allowed to emerge into the open air once the pigs had been disembarked. We might have all died, asphyxiated in our cabins, without anyone caring in the least, as long as there was a pig to disembark or to rescue from sea-sickness.

I am not afraid of the sea, but a member of my family was dangerously ill. The crossing, the foul stench and the lack of sleep had not helped to ease his sufferings. The only attention paid to us by the captain was a request not to put our invalid in the best bed in the cabin, because of a Spanish superstition that every disease is infectious; the captain had already decided to burn the bed in which the invalid slept, he wanted it to be the worst one. We sent him back to his pigs; and a fortnight later, sailing home on board *Le Phénicien*, a magnificent steamer flying our flag, we compared the devoted attention of the Frenchmen with the Spaniard's notion of hospitality. The captain of *El Mallorquin* had grudged a bed to a dying man; the Marseilles captain, believing that our invalid was not comfortable enough, gave him the mattress off his own bed... When I wanted to pay for our passage, the Frenchman observed that I was paying too much; the Majorcan had made me pay the double.

My conclusion is not that man is entirely good in one corner of our *'globe terraqué'*, or entirely bad in another. Moral evil in mankind is the outcome of material misfortune. Suffering engenders fear, mistrust, deceit, every sort of conflict. The Spaniard is ignorant and superstitious; consequently he believes in infection, fears illness and death, lacks in faith and charity. Being miserable and overburdened by taxation he becomes greedy, selfish and deceitful in his dealings with foreigners. History has shown us that whenever he has been given the opportunity to be great, he has displayed greatness; but he is only a man, and where in private life a man must succumb, he succumbs.

I need to lay down this principle before going on to speak of the people such as I found them in Majorca; for I hope I am excused from any further talks on olives, cows and pigs. The length of this last article is not in very good taste. I beg forgiveness from anyone whose feelings may have been hurt by it, and I shall now settle down seriously to my tale. At first I believed that I could follow M. Laurens step by step in his *Artistic Journey*, but I can already see how many different impressions will trouble me as I retrace in memory the rugged footpaths of Majorca.

Chapter IV

'**B**UT if you know nothing about painting,' people will say to me, 'what the devil were you doing aboard that wretched galley?' - I prefer to discuss my family and myself as little as possible; though I shall often be obliged to use the words '*I*' and '*we*'. 'I' and 'we' represent that accidental *subjectivity* without which certain aspects of Majorcan *objectivity*, perhaps interesting to the reader, could not be revealed. I therefore beg everyone to regard my personality as something altogether passive, a telescope for observing scenes in far off lands that recall the proverb: 'I prefer to believe you than go there and see...' Moreover, it is not my wish to regale him with the accidents that happened to me. In recalling them it will be merely as an illustration of a philosophical theme; and once I have formulated my ideas in this respect, I hope the reader will do me the justice of admitting that I am not in the least egocentric.

Without further ado let me tell my reader what I was doing on that galley; in a few words: 'I wanted to travel.' And now it is my turn to ask my reader a question: 'When you travel, dear reader, why do you do it?'

I hear his reply, using the very words I myself would choose: 'I travel for the sake of travelling.'

'I well realize that travel is an end in itself; but still, what impels you to this costly, exhausting and sometimes dangerous pleasure that seems always strewn with innumerable disillusions?'

'The need to travel.'

'Well then, tell me, what is this need? Why does it obsess us all to a greater or lesser degree? Why do we all give way to it, even after realizing time and time again that, as soon as we are in the saddle, the need leaps up behind us and will neither relax its grip on us nor allow us to fully enjoy any place we visit.'

Since my reader has no wish to answer this question, I will take the liberty of doing so myself. In reality, nowhere is any one truly happy, and, that of the many faces assumed by the Ideal - or, if you dislike the word, the concept of something better- travel is one of the most tantalizing and most deceitful. All is rotten in public affairs: those who will not admit to it, feel it more deeply and bitterly than those who assert it. All the same, divine Hope still pursues her way, soothing our troubled hearts with a persistent whisper that there is something better to be found - our ideal.

Our social order does not even command the sympathy of those who defend it, and satisfies no one; each one goes his own way. One throws himself into art, the other into science, and the majority stupefy themselves the best they can. Those of us who have time and money to spare, travel - or perhaps flee; for you surely understand that it is not so much a question of travelling as of getting away? Which of us has not some sorrow to dull, or some yoke to cast off? No one.

Nobody, unless he is completely engrossed in his work or benumbed by laziness, can stay for long in one place without becoming restless and in need of a change. If someone is happy (though only the very great and the very lazy qualify for this title nowadays) he expects to become even happier by travelling; lovers and newly-married couples set out for Switzerland or Italy as do hypochondriacs and idlers. In a word, anyone who feels himself either alive or rotting away is possessed with the fever of the Wandering Jew and rushes off in search of a place for a love-nest, or a place to die.

God forbid that I should declaim against popular migration, or that I envisage a future with men glued to their country, their land, and their house, like polyps to a sponge! Yet if intelligence and morality are to progress simultaneously with industry, railways are clearly not destined to shuttle from one end of the globe to the other entire nations suffering from rancour or morose depression.

I should like to imagine the human race as happier, and therefore peaceful and more enlightened, and leading two parallel lives; the one, a sedentary life devoted to family bliss, work in the city, studious meditation and philosophic contemplation; the other, an active life with an honest exchange which will one day replace the shameful traffic we call commerce, artistic inspiration, scientific research and, above all, the dissemination of ideas. In a word, I believe that the normal aim of travel is a need for contact, communication and the congenial interchange of ideas; duty should always be combined with pleasure. Nowadays, on the contrary, most of us seem to travel in search of mystery and isolation, yet still under the shadow with which the society of our fellow-men cloud all impressions, be they pleasant or unpleasant.

Regarding myself, I set out to satisfy a need for some rest I so desperately needed. Since time is very short in this world that we have made for ourselves, I believed that I should find some remote, quiet retreat where there would be no notes to write, no newspapers to read, no visitors to entertain; where I need never remove my dressing gown and the day would have only twelve hours; where I could shed my obligations to society, isolate myself from the mental turmoil which torments us all in France, and devote a year or two to some historical research, and study my own language afresh with my children.

Who amongst us has not, at some time, selfishly dreamed of forsaking his affairs, his habits, his acquaintances and even his friends, to settle in some enchanted island and live without worries, without responsibilities, and above all, without newspapers?

In all seriousness, it can be said that journalism, (the beginning and the end of everything, as Aesop would have said), has created for man an entirely new life, packed with progress, privileges and preoccupation. This voice of humanity which wakes us up every morning to inform us of how humanity lived yesterday, sometimes proclaiming great truths, sometimes appalling falsehoods, but always marking each step taken by mankind, and striking every hour of social life, is surely a great accomplishment in spite of all the blemishes and faults associated with it?

But though it is necessary for the clarification of our thoughts and our deeds, are we not shocked and bored to see in detail that conflict is everywhere, and that weeks and months roll by accompanied by discord and outrage, without light being thrown on a single question, or any noticeable progress being made? And in this period of waiting, which seems all the longer because each phase is so carefully reported to us, are we not often seized with the desire -we artists who have no control over the helm- to fall asleep on board and not wake up for several years, until we may hail the new land towards which we find ourselves conveyed?

Yes, indeed, if we could escape from communal life and renounce all contact with politics for a while, we would be struck on our return with the progress achieved during our absence. But this is not granted us, and when we flee from the scene of action to seek oblivion and rest amongst a nation whose pace is slower and whose spirit is less fervent than ours, we suffer ills that we could not have foreseen: we regret having left the present for the past, the living for the dead.

This, quite simply, is the theme of my book, and it is my reason for attempting the somewhat unpleasant task of writing it. Although I had promised myself, when I began, to keep my personal feelings as much as possible to myself, I now realize that such an evasion would be cowardly, and consequently retract my promise.

The Interior of the Cathedral. (J. B. Laurens, 1839).

Chapter V

WE arrived in Palma in the month of November, 1838, in
a heat comparable to that of our month of June. We had
left Paris a fortnight before in extremely cold weather, so we
were delighted after experiencing the first onslaughts of winter
to have apparently left the enemy behind. To this pleasure was
added that of exploring a city of great character, and one which
contained several monuments in the first rank of beauty and
rarity.

However, the difficulty in finding accommodation soon
became apparent, and we found the Spaniards who had recommended Majorca to us as a most hospitable island with many
resources had, like ourselves, been under a false illusion. In a
country so close to civilized Europe, we found it difficult to
understand why we were unable to find a single inn. This lack
of even simple accommodation for travellers ought to have warned us from the start how Majorca compared with the rest of
the world, and sent us straight back to Barcelona where, at least,
there is a miserable inn emphatically named the *hôtel des
Quatre-Nations,* the Hotel of the Four Nations.

In Palma one has to be recommended and introduced some
months ahead to twenty of the more important local personages
if one does not want to end up sleeping in the open air. The
most that could be done for us was to secure two small furnish-

ed, or rather semi- furnished, rooms in a disreputable area where a stranger is lucky if he can find a trestle-bed with a mattress a little softer and little more yielding than a slate, a rush chair, and food dominated by peppers and garlic.

In less than an hour we learned that, unless we admitted to being delighted with this reception, we would be looked on with an evil eye for being insolent bunglers or, with better luck, thought of as idiots. Woe betide the traveller in Spain who is not content with all he finds! Make the slightest grimace on finding vermin in a bed, or scorpions in the soup, and you draw upon yourself universal scorn and indignation. So we were careful never to complain, and slowly came to understand the reasons for the lack of comfort and apparent lack of hospitality.

Quite apart from the habitual listlessness and general apathy of the Majorcans, the Civil War, which had for so long raged in Spain, had now severed all communication between the island and the mainland. Majorca had become the refuge of as many Spaniards as it could hold, and the natives, safely entrenched in their homes, were wary of sallying forth in search of adventures and hard knocks in their fatherland.

To add to this, there was the total absence of any industry, and the excessive customs duty levied on all comforts and luxuries.[4] Palma is designed to hold only a certain number of residents, as the population grows they crowd together bit by bit. Few new houses are built. Nothing is altered in their homes; and with the exception of two or three families, the furniture has not

---

[4] For a piano we had sent from France, we had to pay an import duty of 700 francs, which was almost the full value of the instrument. We tried to return it, but this was forbidden; to leave it at the port, pending further instruction, was equally forbidden; to have it moved out of town (we were then living in the country-side) and so at least avoid the harbour dues, which differ from the customs dues, was against the law; to leave it in town and so avoid paying the exit dues, which was distinct from the entrance dues, was also impossible; the only right we had was to hurl it into the sea.

After a fortnight's wrangling we obtained permission to have it taken out of town through a certain gate, instead of being removed through another, and so the whole business was settled for some 400 francs.

changed in two hundred years. They have no idea of fashion, and no need for any luxuries or comforts. They remain blocked in between apathy on the one side and difficulties on the other, and possess no more than is needed for their personal use. Hence hospitality is limited to only words.

There is an expression sacred in Majorca, as in all Spain, if one wants to excuse oneself from lending anything; it consists in offering everything, 'This house and all its contents are at your disposal.' One cannot look at a picture, touch a piece of material, or lift up a chair, without being charmingly told: *"Está a la disposición de Usted."* But beware of accepting so much as a pin, for that would be an intolerable indiscretion.

Shortly after my arrival in Palma, I was guilty of an imprudent error of this kind, after which I believe I will never again rise in the estimation of the Marquis de ***[5]. I had had a most imposing letter of introduction to this young Palma nobleman, and thought that I could accept the loan of his carriage, so charmingly offered, and go for a drive! But the following day a note from the Marquis made me realize that I had contravened all proprieties, and I hastened to return the carriage unused.

Nevertheless, I did come across exceptions to this rule, but only amongst those who had travelled and acquired a knowledge of the world - true cosmopolitans. Even if any of the others, from the goodness of their hearts, felt the need and freedom to offer their help to us, not one of them could have given a corner of their homes to us without experiencing inconveniences and even hardships, (because the high import-dues and the lack of industry have reduced so rich a country to poverty), and we should have been most discourteous in accepting their invitation.

It was in searching for somewhere to settle in, that we began to appreciate their difficulties. In the entire city it was impossible to find a habitable apartment.

---

[5] The Marquis of La Bastida.

An apartment in Palma consists of four bare walls, without doors or windows. In most middle-class houses window panes are not used; and anyone wishing to avail himself of this comfort, essential in winter, must first get the window-frames made. Therefore, when each tenant moves, (and this happens very seldom), he takes the windows, the locks, and even the door-hinges away with him. His successor is obliged to replace these, unless he prefers living in the open air, quite a common custom in Palma.

Now, it takes at least six months to make not only the doors and windows, but also the beds, tables, chairs and all similar furnishings, however plain and primitive. There are very few carpenters; they are not fast workers and their tools and materials are hard to come by; and the Majorcan will always find a good reason not to hurry. Life is long! Only the French, that is to say the extravagant and hysterical, want things done at once. 'If you have waited six months, why not wait another six months? If you don't like the island, why stay? Are you needed here? We can manage quite well without you. And do you think you've come here to turn everything upside down? Oh no, not at all! Of course we'll let you talk, but we do as we please.'

'But have you anything we can hire?'

'Hire? What's this about hiring furniture? Do you believe we have enough to spare for hiring?'

'Or anything for sale?'

'For sale? You mean ready made? Do you think we can afford to make furniture in advance? If you need it, have it sent from France - you can get everything there!'

'But to order it from France, we would have to wait at least six months, and then pay duty on it. So then if one has been foolish enough to come here, the only remedy is to go away again?'

'That is what I should recommend. That, or to have patience, a lot of patience. *Mucha calma,* a sound Majorcan saying.'

We were about to act on this advice, when a well-meaning

person did us the doubtful favour of finding a country house which we could rent.

It was the country home of a rich townsman who, for the price of 100 francs a month, (very moderate by French standards, but high enough by theirs), let us have it as it stood. It was furnished like all country villas: with camp beds or wooden ones painted green, some consisting only of two trestles supporting a couple of boards and a thin mattress; straw-bottomed chairs; rough wooden tables; bare but immaculately whitewashed walls and, the ultimate in luxury, glazed windows in almost every room. Finally, the so-called drawing-room contained four horrible fire-screens, just like those found in our most wretched village inns, which Señor Gomez, our landlord, had been naive enough to have carefully framed, as though they were valuable engravings, to form the mural decorations for his country seat. The villa was vast, airy (too much so), well laid out, and well situated at the base of a mountain slope surrounded by fertile foothills at the far end of a rich valley that runs down to the yellow walls of Palma, the massive cathedral and the sparkling sea on the horizon.

Our first few days in this retreat passed pleasantly. We went for walks, delighting in the lovely weather and a countryside fascinatingly new to us. I had never been very far from my own country, although I have spent a greater part of my life travelling. It was the first time that I saw a land whose vegetation and natural features differed so much to those found in our more temperate latitudes. When I visited Italy and trod the beaches of Tuscany, the grandiose ideas I had of this region prevented me from appreciating its pastoral beauty and smiling grace. On the banks of the Arno, I could well have been walking along the borders of the Indre; and I travelled as far as Venice without finding any reason for emotion or surprise. But in Majorca, I had no place to compare it with. The people, the houses, the vegetation, even the pebbles on the road, had a distinct and special character of their own. My children were so struck by this that

The Market of St. Anthony in Palma. (J. B. Laurens, 1839).

they collected everything, and tried to fill our trunks with those beautiful blocks of quartz and multi-coloured veined marble which are found in the dry stone walls of every enclosure. The peasants, who saw us collecting even dead twigs, mistook us for apothecaries, others for simple idiots.

Son Vent in Establiments. (Pub. by J. Hetzel. Paris, 1856).

Chapter VI

T HE island offers a rich variety of landscape which resulted from the cataclysms and the laboured and continuous movements of the earth that had taken place in a primeval world. From the place where we were now living, called Establiments, the extensive horizon of a few leagues enclosed a widely differing scenery.

Surrounding us, and following the contours of the foothills that merged with the fertile plain, the farmed land was confined to a system of broad, irregular terraces. This method of cultivating terraces, common throughout the island which is under the constant threat of rain and sudden torrential floods, favours the growth of trees and gives the island the appearance of a well kept orchard.

To the right, the hills progressively rose from the gentle sloping pastures to the pine covered mountains. In the winter, and occasionally after summer thunderstorms, a small stream runs at the foot of these mountains, though when we arrived it was nothing more than a bed of jumbled rocks. But the lovely mosses which overgrew the stones; the little bridges, coated green by the damp, cracked by the force of currents and half hidden by the branches of willows and poplars; these slender, intertwining, leafy trees overhung and cradled the river-bed in greenery from bank to bank; the meagre trickle of water flowed soundlessly amongst the reeds and the myrtles, and the ever present group of children, women and goats mustered on the mysterious embankments, made this a perfect setting for a painter. We took daily walks along the river bed, and we called it 'Poussin's Corner' because this wild, melancholic yet elegant corner of the landscape reminded us of all that which the great master so particularly cherished.

A hundred yards or so from our refuge, the stream split into several rivulets and seemed to lose itself in the plain. The olive and carob trees spread their branches above the cultivated land, giving it the appearance of a wood.

On many of the round hillocks surrounding this wooded area several imposing houses, although really Lilliputian in size, were to be seen. One could never believe how many barns, sheds, stables, yards and gardens a *pagés* (peasant) manages to accumulate into an acre of land, and what innate good taste presides over this apparently whimsical lay-out. The cottages usually consist of two storeys with a flat roof. The eaves project, protecting a perforated gallery, resembling as it were a row of battlements in the Florentine style. This symmetrical crown lends an air of splendour and strength to even the most fragile and poor of buildings, and huge sheaves of maize hanging at every opening of the gallery form a garland of alternating amber and red, giving an unbelievingly rich and opulent effect. Each cottage is usually surrounded by a strong hedge of cactus, or nopal, whose peculiar racquet-shaped growths intertwine to wall off and protect the frail reed and cane sheep pens from the cold winds. Since these peasants never rob one another, this is the only type of barrier that encloses their properties. Massive almond and orange trees surround the gardens where hardly any other vegetables other than tomatoes and red peppers grow; but all this is wonderfully coloured, and often, to set off the picture, a solitary palm tree unfolds its elegant parasol, or gracefully leans over like the feather-plume of a hat.

This region is in one of the most prosperous districts of Majorca, and the reasons given by M. Grasset de Saint-Sauveur in his *Journey to the Balearic Islands* confirm my remarks about the shortcomings in general of Majorcan agriculture. The observations made by this government official regarding the apathy and ignorance of the local *pagés*, led him to investigate their causes. He found two main ones.

The first was the great number of monasteries which absorbed a large portion of the limited population. This obstacle has disappeared, thanks to M. Mendizábal's drastic decree; and for which the devout and pious Majorcans will never forgive him.

The second was the prevailing spirit of servitude which landed scores of people in the service of the rich and the nobility. This evil still abounds. Every Majorcan aristocrat has a more numerous retinue than he can afford to retain, and derives little benefit from it; it is impossible to be worse attended than by these honorary servants. When one asks on what a rich Majorcan spends his income in a country lacking all luxuries and temptations, the answer is to be found in a specially set aside wing of his house, filled with good-for-nothing loafers of both sexes, who after spending a year in service to their master, have the right to be lodged, clothed and boarded for the rest of their lives. Those who wished to leave the service could do so by foregoing some benefits; but custom permitted them their continued morning visits to take chocolate with their one-time comrades, and, like Sancho in Camacho's house, to share in all household feasts.

At first sight these customs appear patriarchal, and one is prone to admire the republican spirit governing the relations between master and servant; but one soon recognizes it as an ancient Roman form of Republicanism, and that these servants are shackled by indolence and penury to the vanity of their masters. In Majorca it is a luxury to have fifteen servants in an establishment where two would suffice. And when one sees vast stretches of untilled land, industry in ruin, and all progress proscribed by stupidity and sloth, one is at a loss to know who deserves the greater contempt; the master who encourages and perpetuates the moral debasement of his fellow-beings, or the slave who prefers idle degradation to work which would help him recover an independence consonant with human dignity.

It happened once that certain rich Majorcan landowners, noting that their expenses were increasing and their income was waning, decided on a remedy to cure the laziness of their workers and the shortage of labour. They leased part of their estates to their peasants on a life tenure, and M. Grasset de Saint Sauveur observed that, on the great estates wherever this measure was tried, apparently barren land suddenly produced an abundance in the hands of men determined to improve it; and that after a few years both contracting parties had prospered substantially.

In this respect, M. Grasset's predictions have been fully realized, and today the district of Establiments, among others, has become an extensive garden; many new homes have been built on the hillocks, and the peasants have acquired a reasonable standard of living, which, though it has not fully enlightened them, has increased their working capacity. It will be many years before the Majorcan becomes energetic and industrious; and, if like us, he must first pass through the painful stage of yearning to become rich quickly before learning that this is not the goal of humanity, we can meanwhile leave him to pass the time with his guitar and his rosary. But, without doubt, a better fate than ours lies in store for these young nations, whom we are destined to initiate into true civilization without reminding them of what we have done for them. They are not strong enough to face the revolutionary storms which our yearning for perfection has brought down upon our heads. Alone, disowned, mocked and condemned by the rest of the world, we have taken enormous strides ahead; yet the noise of our gigantic struggles has not broken the profound slumber of these small nations who sleep within range of our cannons in the heart of the Mediterranean.

The day will come when we shall confer on the them the baptism of true liberty, and they will share in the feast, like labourers of the twelfth hour. Let us discover the meaning of our social destiny; let us realize our exalted dreams; and while surrounding nations gradually enter into our revolutionary church, these unfortunate islanders, whose weaknesses lay them at the mercy of predatory nations, will flock to join our communion.

Until the day comes when we shall be the first in Europe to decree equality for all men and independence for all nations, the world will be ruled by the strongest armies and the craftiest diplomats; the rights of the people is a mere phrase, and the only prospect facing such isolated minorities as

The Transylvanian, Turk or Magyar [6]

is to be devoured by the conqueror.

If it were always to be so, I should not wish Spain, England or even France to be the guardian of Majorca, but should take as little interest in the fortuitous issue of events as I take in the odd brand of civilization that we are now introducing into Africa.

---

[6]   La Fontaine: *'Fable of the Thieves and the Ass'*

Chapter VII

W E had spent three weeks in Establiments before the rains came. Until then the weather had been enchanting; the lemon trees and the myrtles were still in flower, and once, in early December, I stayed out on a terrace until five o'clock in the morning, enjoying the delightful warm air. You may believe me when I say the temperature was high because I know no one who feels the cold as much as I do, and all my enthusiasm for the beauties of Nature vanishes at the first sign of chilliness. Besides, despite of the delight of the moonlit landscape and the perfume of the flowers which reached up to me, my vigil was not an exacting one. I was there, not as a poet in search of inspiration, but as an idler, looking and listening.

As we all know, it is a commonly accepted fact that each country has its harmonies, its discords, its cries, its mysterious murmurings, and this language of material things is by no means the least of the distinctive signs which impress the traveller. The mysterious lapping of water against the cold marble surfaces, the heavy measured steps of the *sbirros* on the quay, the piercing and almost childlike cry of field-mice chasing one another and quibbling on the muddy flagstones, in short all the furtive and curious noises that faintly disturb the gloomy silence of a Venetian night, bear no resemblance whatsoever to the monotonous sound of the sea, the *¿quien vive?* (who goes there?)

of the sentries, and the melancholy chant of the *serenos* (night-watchmen) of Barcelona. The harmonies of Lake Maggiore are different to those of the Lake of Geneva. The perpetual crackling of fir-cones in the Swiss forests bears no resemblance to the crackling heard on the glaciers.

In Majorca the silence is deeper than anywhere else. The asses and mules who spend the night at pasture interrupt it occasionally by shaking their bells, which have a less deep but more melodious tone than those worn by Swiss cows. The music of the *bolero* reverberates in the loneliest places and on the darkest of nights. There is no peasant who does not have a guitar and who does not take it with him at any hour. From my terrace I could also hear the sea, but so distant and so faint that the strangely fantastic and remarkable poem of Djins came to my mind:

J'écoute,	*I listen*
Tout fuit.	*Everything flees.*
On doute,	*One hesitates,,*
La nuit,	*At night,*
Tout passe;	*All passes by;*
L'espace	*Distance*
Efface	*Erases*
Le bruit.	*Noise*

On a neighbouring farm I could hear a child crying. I could also hear his mother lulling him to sleep with a lovely native air, rather monotonous, rather sad and very Arabic. But other less poetic voices came to remind me of the ludicrous side of Majorca.

The pigs woke up and started grunting in a way that I am at a loss to define. Then the *pagés*, the paterfamilias, was awakened by the voice of his beloved pigs, as the mother had been roused by the cries of her baby. I heard him put his head out of the window and scold the inhabitants of the sty in forceful tones. The pigs understood him perfectly, for they fell silent. Then the *pagés,* apparently with the hope of falling asleep again, recited his rosary in a gloomy voice which, according as drowsiness came and went, receded or rose again like the distant murmur of the waves. From time to time the pigs still let loose a savage grunt; whereupon the *pagés* would raise his voice without interrupting his prayer, and the docile beasts, relaxed by an *Ora pro nobis* or an *Ave Maria* recited in a particular manner, grew quiet once more. As for the child, he was doubtlessly listening, eyes wide open, lost in the stupor into which the nascent mind of cradled humanity, destined to perform mysterious labours within itself before revealing itself, is plunged by unexplained noises.

But suddenly, after these tranquil nights, the weather broke. Awakening one morning, after the wind had wailed lullabies all night and the rain had beaten on our windows, we heard the noise of the torrent which had begun to push its way through the stones of its bed. The next morning, it was louder; and two days later the water was rolling over the boulders that lay in its path. All the blossoms had fallen from the trees, and water was streaming into the ill-protected rooms of our house.

The lack of precaution taken by the Majorcans against the scourges of the wind and rain is incomprehensible. Their delusion or their bravado is so great in this respect, that they flatly deny the existence of these fortuitous, if serious, variations in climate. Until the very end of the two months of downpour which we had to withstand, they insisted that it never rained in Majorca. Yet, had we carefully observed the position of the mountain peaks, and taken into account the direction of the prevailing winds, we would have realized well beforehand the inevitable hardships that the winter must entail.

But another ordeal lay in store for us; it is the one which I have already referred to when I, at last, started describing my journey. One of our group fell ill. Being very delicate and subject to a serious inflammation of the larynx, he was soon affected by the dampness. The House of the Wind (*Son Vent* in Majorcan), the name of the house we were renting from Señor

Chopin and Maurice at Son Vent. Drawing by Maurice Sand.

Gomez, became uninhabitable. The walls were so thin that the lime, with which our rooms had been whitewashed, swelled up like a sponge. Never have I suffered so much from the cold, although the temperatures were not so low; but, for people like us who are used to keeping warm in the winter, in this house without a fireplace, where the damp fell like a cloak of ice over our shoulders, I felt paralysed.

We could not accustom ourselves to the asphyxiating smell of the braziers, and our invalid began to suffer and to cough.

From this moment we became an object of horror and fear to the villagers. We were tried and convicted on a charge of pulmonary consumption which, according to the prejudiced view of Spanish medicine, is as contagious as the bubonic plague. A wealthy doctor, who for the modest fee of 45 francs, consented to visit us, declared that nothing was wrong and did not suggest anything. We gave him the nickname of *Malvavisco* (marshmallow) because of his single prescription.

Another doctor came obligingly to our help; but the pharmacy in Palma was so bare that we could obtain only the most loathsome of drugs. Moreover, the illness seems to have been aggravated by causes which neither science nor devotion could effectively combat.

One morning, when we were greatly disturbed by the persistence of these rains and by the worries directly and indirectly caused by them, we received a letter from the coarse Gomez, informing us, in Spanish style, that we were *sheltering* a person, who was *harbouring* a disease, which was likely to infect his house, and constituted a threat to his family; by virtue of this he requested us to clear out of his place as soon as possible.

This caused us little regret, for we could not have stayed there much longer without being drowned in our rooms; but our invalid was in no condition to be moved without danger, especially bearing in mind the type of transport available in Mallorca and the state of the weather. Besides, the problem was where to go; for the news of our consumption had spread

Son Vent (Establiments). Drawing by Maurice Sand.

rapidly, and we had not the slightest chance of finding lodging, not even if we paid in gold and only stayed for a single night. We were well aware that any considerate person who would offer to take us in would be open to prejudice, and that by accepting such an offer, they would be burdened with the condemnation which weighed upon us. But for the hospitality of the French Consul, who worked miracles to harbour us all under his roof, we should have been obliged to camp in some cave like proper gypsies.

Another miracle happened, and we found a home for the winter. A Spanish political refugee had gone into hiding in the Carthusian monastery of Valldemosa. While visiting the Charterhouse we had been struck by his refined bearing, his wife's melancholic beauty, and the rustic furnishings of their cell. The poetic atmosphere of this monastery went to my head. It turned out that this mysterious couple wanted to hurriedly leave the country, and they were as delighted to hand over their furnished cell to us as we were to acquire it. So for the fair sum of one thousand francs, we came into possession of a fully furnished household; this was very reasonable (though in France it would have only cost us some hundred crowns), for simple and essential goods are rare, costly and difficult to come by in Majorca.

As we now spent four days in Palma, during which time I hardly left the fireplace which the Consul had the good fortune to possess (the deluge still continued), I shall interrupt my narrative here with a brief description of the capital of Majorca. I shall now present to the reader M. Laurens, who came in the following year to explore and sketch its most beautiful aspects, as a guide, for he is far more versed in archaeology than I am.

Part Two

The Arab Baths. (J. B. Laurens, 1839).

Chapter I

A LTHOUGH Majorca was occupied for four hundred years by the Moors, few relics of their occupation survive. The only remains in Palma are the Arab Baths.

There are no Roman remains, and there are a few Carthaginian ruins to be found near Alcudia, their ancient capital, and the tradition of Hannibal's birth, which M. Gasset de Saint-Sauveur attributes to the overweening conceit of the Majorcan, although this account is not entirely unbelievable.[7]

Yet the Arab style survives in the smallest constructional details, and it has been necessary for M. Laurens to correct the archeological errors of his predecessors, lest ignorant travellers like myself should think they were discovering authentic traces of Moorish architecture at every step.

'I saw no houses in Palma,' says M.Laurens, 'which seemed to be very old. The most interesting as regards architecture and antiquity date from the begining of the sixteenth century; but the exquisite and brilliant art of that period was not expressed in the same manner as in France.

'These houses have only one storey above the ground floor

---

[7] The Majorcans claim that Hamilcar, on his way from Africa to Catalonia with his pregnant wife, stopped at a point on the island to visit a temple dedicated to Lucina, Goddess of Childbirth, and that Hannibal was born there. The same account is to be found in the *History of Majorca* by Dameto. (Grasset de Saint-Sauveur.)

and a low attic.[8] The street entrance consists of an unadorned arch; but the size and the great number of stones radiating outwards from it, makes a most impressive facade. Light enters the spacious rooms of the first floor through tall windows divided by exceedingly slender columns, lending them a thoroughly Moorish look.

'This feature is so strongly pronounced that I felt obliged to visit more than twenty houses built in the same style to investigate every detail of their structure, before I could convince myself that these windows had not been removed from the walls of some enchanted Moorish palace, of which the Alhambra at Granada is a surviving example.

'Only in Majorca have I found six foot high columns having a diameter of only three inches. The fine quality of their marble and the style of their capitals crowning them, led me to believe they had an Arabic origin. Be that as it may, these windows are as lovely as the originals.

'The top floor attic is in the form of a gallery, with a row of window openings imitating those which crown the *Lonja*. Lastly, a projecting roof, supported by finely carved beams, protects this floor from rain and sun, and creates lively patterns of light and shade by casting long shadows on the house and contrasts the brownish block of the masonry with the brightness of the sky.

'The staircase, a work of great refinement, rises from the courtyard in the centre of the house, and is separated from the street entrance by a vestibule, remarkable for the capitals of its columns which are decorated either with carved foliage or with an insignia supported by angels.

'For more than a century after the Renaissance, the Majorcans lavished a great deal of money on the building of their private homes. Whilst always maintaining the same layout, they adapted current fashions to their vestibules and staircases.

---

[8] They were not true attics, but more like drying-rooms, locally known as *porchos*.

Hence one finds everywhere Tuscan or Doric columns; and the ornate ramps and balustrades lend a sumptuous look to these aristocratic mansions.

'This love for ornate staircases and the Moorish touch is to be found even in the most humble of homes, where a single steep flight of steps leads straight from the street to the first floor. There, each step is faced with earthenware tiles decorated with bright flowers in blue, yellow or red.'

This description is most accurate, and the drawings by M. Laurens successfully reproduce the elegance of these interiors, whose peristyles would provide us with beautifully simple stage sets.

These small paved courtyards are sometimes surrounded by columns resembling the *cortile* of Venetian palaces, and have a simply designed well in the centre. They neither look like, nor serve the same purpose as, our own dirty bare courtyards. They never give access to stables and coach-houses. They are authentic courtyards, reminiscent of the Roman *atrium*. The central well clearly evolves from the *impluvium*.

When these peristyles are decorated with pots of flowers and reed mats, their combined elegance and severity result in a poetic charm that is quite lost on the Majorcan aristocrats, who never cease to apologize for the antiquity of their homes; and when you admire the style, they smile, believing you are making fun of them and perhaps secretly despising this ridiculous excess of French courtesy.

Moreover, not everything in these mansions of the Majorcan nobility is as poetic as their entrances. There are certain unhygenic details that embarrass me greatly to describe, unless I could do so in Latin, like Jaquemont when he is discussing Indian customs.

But not knowing Latin, I must refer the curious to the passage which M. Grasset, a less responsible writer than M. Laurens, but very truthful on this point, devotes to the condition of larders found in Majorca, as well as those in the old houses of Spain and Italy. It is a remarkable passage, especially regarding a curious Spanish medical prescription which is still very popular in Majorca.[9]

The insides of these palaces do not correspond at all to the outsides. Nothing is more revealing, whether one is considering the question of nationality or individuality, than the arrangement and furnishing of the home.

In Paris, where the vagaries of fashion and the abundance of manufactured goods allow remarkable differences in the aspects of apartments, it suffices to enter a well-to-do person's home to gain a quick idea of his character. It is immediately obvious whether he is a person of taste and orderliness, or is greedy or careless, or whether he has a tidy mind or a romantic one, or is hospitable or pretentious.

Like most, I have my own system of judgement which, I must admit, does not always prevent me from drawing false conclusions.

I have a great horror of a sparsely furnished and scrupulously tidy room. Unless the occupant is one of great intelligence and noble of heart, transcending all material issues, allowing him to consider his home as a mere shelter, I believe him to have an empty head and a cold heart.

I cannot understand those who, while living between four walls, feel no need to furnish these, be it only with logs and baskets, and to have something alive around them, if only a wretched flower or a miserable sparrow.

Emptiness and stillness terrify me, symmetry and stern order fill me with despair; If my imagination could accept the idea of eternal damnation, my hell would certainly be to have to live for ever in a provincial house where order reigns supreme, where nothing is ever moved, where nothing is ever left lying about, where nothing is ever worn out or broken, where no animal is admitted on the pretext that the animate damage the inanimate. Destroy all the carpets in the world, if the only

9 Grasset de Saint Sauveur, p. 119.

"Can Olesa", the home of a noble Majorcan. (J. B. Laurens, 1839).

way for me to enjoy them is never to see a child, a cat or dog cavorting over them!

Such austere orderliness does not derive from a true love to cleanliness, but either from extreme laziness or from a sordid sense of economy. With moderate care, the kindly housekeeper of my choice would keep our home in a state of cleanliness indispensable to our comfort.

But what can one say of a family whose home is void and static without even having the excuse of cleanliness?

Though one may be mistaken, as I have just said, regarding individual instances, one is rarely mistaken in general cases. A person's character is revealed by their customs and their furnishings, as much as in their features and their language.

Having combed Palma in search of rooms, I entered a fair number of houses. They all looked so much alike that I could only deduce general characteristics common to the occupants. I never entered one of the houses without the feeling of distress and boredom at the sight of those bare walls, those dusty and stained flagstones and the sparse and dirty furniture. It all bore witness to indifference and inaction; no book was to be seen, no handiwork either. The men did not read, the women did not sew. The only sign of domestic activity was the smell of garlic from the kitchen; and the only traces of private entertainment were cigar butts strewn on the floor.

This lack of intellectual activity gives a house a lifelessness and an emptiness unlike anything we have at home, and makes the Majorcan appear more African than European.

Thus, all these dwellings, where generation followed generation without making the least change to their environment, or without leaving any individual imprint on things which normally form part of daily human life, reminded me of caravanserais rather than proper homes; and while ours give the feeling of a family nest, theirs resemble refuges where groups of wanderers gather to pass the night. People who know Spain well, have told me that this holds good for the whole of the Peninsula.

So, coming back to what I mentioned before, the peristyle, or *atrium*, of mansions owned by the *Cavallers* (as the nobility of Majorca like to call themselves) has a great feeling of hospitality and even comfort. But after climbing the elegant staircase and entering the house itself, you might think that you have entered an area dedicated solely to the *siesta*. Vast rooms, usually rectangular in shape, very high, very cool, very dark , wholly bare, whitewashed, with enormous old portraits blackened with age, hung in single row so high up that that one could distinguish nothing; four or five greasy, worm-eaten leather chairs bordered with great gilded studs that have not been polished in two hundred years; a few Valencian mats, or long-haired sheepskins thrown here and there on the paving; highly set casement windows covered by heavy curtains; huge wooden doors of the same black oak used in the beamed ceiling, and sometimes an antique gold door-curtain bearing the richly embroidered family coat of arms, but tarnished and worn away by age; such are the interiors of Majorcan palaces. No tables are to be seen except the dining table; mirrors are a rarity, and occupy so small an area in their massive frames, that they cast hardly any light.

The master of the house will be found standing and smoking in deep silence, the mistress will be seated in a huge chair, playing with her fan and thinking of nothing. One never sees the children; they live with the servants in the kitchen, or in the attic, I do not know which; the parents do not bother about them. A chaplain comes and goes, doing nothing. The twenty or thirty servants take their siesta, while a churlish maid opens the door at the visitor's fifteenth ring of the bell.

This sort of life is certainly not lacking in *character*, as we would say, taking into consideration the broader meaning that we have given to this word nowadays; but even if the most placid member of our middle-class were condemned to live this way, he would be driven mad with despair or spiritual reaction would soon make a demagogue of him.

Chapter II

T HE three most important buildings in Palma are the Cathedral, the Lonja (Exchange), and the Royal Palace. The Cathedral, attributed by the Majorcans to James the Conqueror, their first Christian king and as it were their Charlemagne, was in effect begun under his reign, though not finished until 1601. It is starkly massive; the limestone used throughout is of a very fine texture and has a lovely amber colour.

This imposing mass, which stands on the seashore, has a tremendous impact on the visitor as he enters the harbour; but in reality, the only remarkable feature is the southern portal, which M. Laurens describes as the finest specimen of Gothic architecture he had ever had the opportunity of drawing. The interior is extremely austere and sombre.

Because sea winds blew with such force through large openings and through the main door shaking the pictures and holy vessels during services, all the doorways and rose-windows on this side have now been bricked up. The nave measures no less than five hundred and forty palms[10] in length and seventy-five in width.

In the centre of the choir stands a very simple marble sarcophagus, which is opened to show visitors the mummified

[10] The Spanish *palmo* is equivalent to the *pan* of our French southern provinces.

body of James II, son of the Conqueror, a devout prince, as weak and gentle as his father had been bold and warlike.

The Majorcans claim that their Cathedral is far superior to that of Barcelona and that their Lonja is infinitely more beautiful than that of Valencia - I have never verified the latter assertion and the former cannot be substantiated.

In both cathedrals the grotesque trophy characteristic of Spanish provincial capitals is displayed: the gruesome turbaned head of a Moor in painted wood, forming the end of the pendentive of the organ. This image of a severed head is often decorated with a long white beard, splashed with red paint from below to show the tainted blood of the conquered.

One sees many coats of arms emblazoned on the keystones of the aisle arches. To have their escutcheons in the House of God was a privilege for which the Majorcan Cavallers paid highly; and it is thanks to this tax on their vanity that the Cathedral could be completed in a century when religious devotion had somewhat cooled. It would be very unjust to attribute the Majorcans alone with a weakness which in that epoch was common with all the religious aristocracy of the world.

The Lonja, with its elegant proportions and its character of originality which does not impede a faultless and simple symmetry in good taste, is the building which impressed me most profoundly.

This Exchange was begun and finished during the first half of the fifteenth century. The famous Jovellanos described it in great detail, and several years ago the *Magasin Pittoresque* popularized it with a very interesting drawing. The interior is a vast hall supported by six elegant spirally fluted columns.

Intended originally as a meeting place for merchants and seafarers who flocked to Palma, the Lonja now attests the lost splendours of Majorcan commerce; today it is reserved for the celebration of public festivals. It would have been interesting to see the Majorcans, dressed in the sumptuous costumes of their forefathers, disporting themselves soberly in this ancient ball-

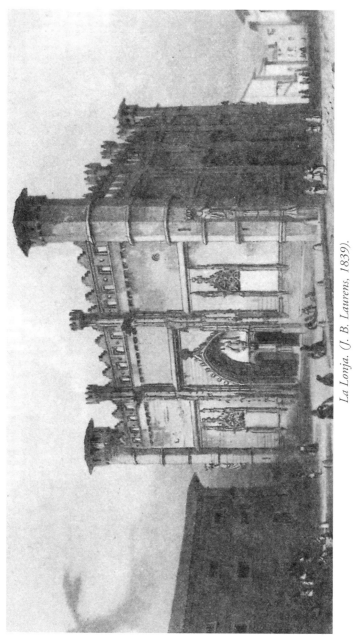

La Lonja. (J. B. Laurens, 1839).

room; but rain kept us captive on the mountain, and we were unable to see this carnival, less famous and perhaps less gloomy than that of Venice. Nevertheless, the Lonja, as lovely as it may be, it can never erase my memory of that exquisite jewel called the Cadora, the old mint on the Grand Canal.

The Royal Palace of Palma, which M. Grasset de Saint-Sauveur does not hesitate to describe as Romanesque and Moorish (this inspired him with feelings quite in keeping with the First Empire), is said to have been built in 1309. M. Laurens declares that his conscience was troubled by the placing of the small twin windows, and the puzzling colonettes which he studied there.

Would it be rash to attribute the anomalies of style that are found in so many Majorcan buildings to the inclusion of old fragments in later buildings? Just as, in France and Italy, the Renaissance taste incorporated original Greek and Roman medallions and bas-reliefs in sculptural ornamentation, is it not possible that Majorcan christians, after having torn down all Moorish[11] monuments, made use of that rich debris by using it in their later constructions?

Be that as it may, the Royal Palace of Palma has a very picturesque appearance. There is nothing more unsymmetrical,

---

[11] The capture and sacking of Palma by the Christians on the 31st of December 1229, is strikingly described in the *Chronicle of Marsigli* (hitherto unpublished). Here is an extract:

'The plunderers and thieves who ransacked the houses found in them the most beautiful Moorish women and girls, whose laps were filled with gold and silver coins, pearls and precious stones, gold and silver bracelets, sapphires and every kind of costly jewel. They showed all these things to the armed men who appeared before them and, crying bitterly, they said to them in Saracen: "All these are yours, but leave us only enough to live on."

'Such was their greed for profit, such the disintegration of self control, that the men of the royal house of Aragon, immersed in their search for hidden valuables, did not appear before their King for eight days.

'It had come to such a point that, since neither the cook nor any servant of the royal household could be found, an Arogonese nobleman, Ladro, said:

"- Sire, I invite you to eat with me, for I have plenty, and I am told there is a fine cow at my abode; there you may eat and sleep tonight."

'The King was most delighted and followed the said nobleman.'

The Royal Palace of Palma. (J. B. Laurens, 1839).

more inconvenient, more uncivilized and more mediaeval; it is proud, full of character and very noble, a manor composed of galleries, towers, terraces and archways that climb one on top of another to reach a considerable height, and culminating in a Gothic angel who, from the heart of the clouds, gazes across the sea to Spain.

This Palace, which stores all the archives, is the residence of the Captain-General, the most important man on the island. This is how M. Grasset de Saint-Sauveur describes the interior of this residence:

'The first room is a type of vestibule that serves as a guard-house. To the right there are two huge chambers, where there is hardly a chair to be found.

'The third room is the audience-chamber, containing a crimson velvet throne fringed with gold and placed on a dias three steps high and covered by a carpet. On either side stand two lions of gilded wood. The canopy over the throne is made of the same crimson velvet and crowned by ostrich plumes. Portraits of the King and Queen hang above the throne.

'It is in this chamber, on ceremonial occasions or gala days, that the General receives representatives of the various branches of the civil service, the garrison officers, and high ranking foreigners.'

The Captain-General, who acted as Governor, honoured us by receiving in this chamber the one[12] who undertook to present our letters of introduction. Our companion found this top functionary near his throne, which most certainly was the same one as described by Grasset de Saint-Sauveur in 1807; it was worn, faded, threadbare and stained with oil and candle wax. Although the two lions were no longer gilded, they still grimaced ferociously. Only the royal effigy had changed; this time it was the innocent Isabel who, like a monstrous inn-sign, filled the ancient gilt frame where her august forefathers had succeed-

---

12 Chopin. *(Translator's note.)*

ed one another, rather like models in an art-school frame. The Governor, despite being housed like Hoffman's Duke of Irénéus, was none the less a man of high esteem and princely graciousness.

A fourth and very interesting building is the Palace of the City Hall, dating from the sixteenth century, which is with reason, comparable to the palaces of Florence. Its roof is remarkable for the projecting eaves, reminiscent of the Florentine palaces or Swiss chalets; moreover, it has the unusual feature of being supported by wooden caissons, lavishly carved with rosettes and alternating with tall caryatids which extend out beneath the eaves, groaning under the weight, for most of them have their faces hidden in their hands.

I have never seen the inside of this building, which houses a collection of portraits of Majorcan celebrities. Among these eminent personages, one sees the renowned Don Jaime[13], portrayed as the *King of Diamonds*. There is also an ancient painting depicting the funeral of the enlightened Majorcan scholar Ramon Llull and it also shows a most varied array of ancient costumes worn by people in the funeral cortege. Finally, in this municipal building, there is a superb *St. Sebastian* by Van Dyck, the existence of which no one in Majorca thought fit to tell me.

'Palma has an art-school,' adds M. Laurens, 'which has already produced, in this nineteenth century alone, some thirty-six painters, eight sculptors, eleven architects and six engravers, all of them masters of their craft - if we are to believe the *Dictionary of Famous Majorcan Artists*, recently published by the learned Antonio Furió.' I must quite frankly confess that during my stay in Palma I never realized that I was surrounded by so many great men, for I saw nothing that led me to guess their existence...

'Some rich families own a few paintings from the Spanish School... However, should you look in the shops, and if you visit the home of an ordinary citizen, you will find nothing more

[13] King James of Aragon. *(Translator's note.)*

than coloured prints of the sort that hawkers sell in our market places, and which in France would only be found in the home of a poor and simple peasant.'

The most celebrated palace in Palma is that of the Count of Montenegro, one of the leading figures in Majorca, now an old man in his eighties, formerly Captain-General, one of the most illustrious by birth and one of the wealthiest on the island.

This gentleman has a library which we were permitted to visit, but I did not open a single book there and I was unable to pronounce a word (so great is my respect for books that it almost amounts to fear) had not a learned compatriot of mine informed me of the importance of the treasures before which I had so thoughtlessly passed, like the fable of the cock that ignored the pearls.

This fellow countryman, M. Tastu[14], had spent almost two years in Catalonia and Majorca on a study of the Romance languages. He kindly lent me his notes, and, with a generosity very rare among scholars, permitted me to make whatever use of them I liked. I shall not do so without warning my reader that this traveller was as enthusiastic about all things Majorcan as I had been disappointed.

In order to explain this difference of impressions, I could say that during my stay, the Majorcans were uncomfortably packed together so as to make room for some twenty thousand Spaniards who had fled the war, so it may not have been due to oversight or prejudice that I found Palma inhabitable and the Majorcans less ready, than two years before, to welcome a new surplus of foreigners. But I would prefer to incur the disapproval of some considerate person who will correct me, rather than narrate impressions I have not experienced.

Therefore, I would be very happy to be publicly contradicted and reprimanded, as I have been in private; for the public would gain an accurate and far more interesting book on

---

[14] M. Tastu, one of our most erudite linguists, and married to one of our most talented and most noble Muses.

Majorca than this disconnected and perhaps unjust version I am compelled to give.

So let M. Tastu publish his account of his journey; I swear that I shall read with great pleasure anything that may change my opinion of the Majorcans. I have known a few whom I should like to consider as representatives of the general type and who, I hope, will never doubt my feelings regarding them, should this book ever fall into their hands.

M. Tastu mentions, in his notes on the intellectual riches of Majorca, the Count of Montenegro's library; I went through it so casually in the company of the house Chaplain, being more interested in the interior of this old bachelor nobleman's home. It was a sad and gloomy home, silently ruled by a priest.

'This library,' M. Tastu writes, 'was created by the Count of Montenegro's uncle, Cardinal Antonio Despuig, an intimate friend of Pope Pius VI.

'The learned Cardinal gathered everything of bibliographical interest that was to be found in Spain, Italy and France. The section dealing with numismatology and the ancient arts, is remarkably complete.

'Among the small number of manuscripts it holds, is one of great interest to students of calligraphy: a Book of Hours. The miniatures are exquisite, the best of its period.

'Students of heraldry will find an Armorial with the coats of arms of the Spanish nobility correctly drawn and coloured, including those of noble families from Aragon, Majorca, Roussillon and Languedoc. The manuscript, which appears to date from the sixteenth century, belonged to the Dameto family, who are related to the Despuigs and the Montenegros. Paging through it, we came across the coat of arms of the *Bonapart* family, from which our great Napoleon descended, of which we made a *fac-simile* which we shall see further on...

'In this library there is also a beautiful nautical chart made by the Majorcan Valseca, dating from 1439. It is a masterpiece of calligraphy and topography, and beautifully finished with gems of miniature art. This map had once belonged to Amerigo Vespucci, who had paid a remarkably high price for it, as is affirmed by a contemporary inscription on the back: *Questa ampla pelle di geographia fù pagata da Amerigo Vespucci CXXX ducati di oro di marco.*

'This valuable example of mediaeval geography will soon be published as a sequel to the Catalan-Majorcan Atlas of 1375, and inserted in Volume XIV, Part 2 of the 'Manuscripts noted by the Academy of Inscriptions and Belles Lettres'.'

As I transcribe the above passage, my hair stands on end as I recall a terrible scene. We were in Montenegro's Library, and the Chaplain was unrolling before us this very same nautical chart, this rare and precious treasure for which Amerigo Vespucci had paid 130 gold ducats, and God knows how much the amateur antiquarian Cardinal Despuig paid!.. when one of the Count's forty or fifty servants had the bright idea of placing a cork ink-well on one of the corners of the parchment to keep it open on the table. The inkwell was full, but full to the brim!

The parchment, used to being rolled up, and perhaps pos-sessed by some wicked spirit, moved, crackled, jumped, and rolled up on itself, taking the inkwell with it. There was a great outcry and the Chaplain turned paler than the parchment itself.

They slowly unrolled the map, hoping that no damage had been done. Alas! The inkwell was empty. The map was inunda-ted, and the beautifully painted miniatures of the kings were sailing in a sea literally blacker than the Euxine.

Panic broke out and I believe that the Chaplain fainted. The servants rushed up with buckets of water, as if a fire had broken out, and began to furiously mop and wipe the map with spon-ges and brushes, washing away kings, seas, islands and conti-nents.

Before we could restrain their zeal, the chart was partially damaged, but fortunately, and thanks to M. Tastu who had made an accurate tracing of it, will be to some extent reparable.

But how great must have been the Chaplain's consternation

when his master learned of the mishap! We were some six feet from the table at the moment of the accident; but I am certain that the whole weight of blame for this deed was placed on the French, and this has not helped to improve our standing in Majorca.

This tragic event prevented us from admiring or even noticing any of the other treasures in the Palace of Montenegro: the show-case of medals, the antique bronzes, the paintings. We were anxious to flee before the Count returned; and certain that we would be accused of this mishap, we did not dare to return. Therefore, to correct my ignorance, I shall resort to the notes of M. Tastu.

'Adjoining the Cardinal's library is a show-case of Celtiberian, Moorish, Greek, Roman and mediaeval medallions; a priceless collection, now in a lamentable state of disorder, waiting for a scholar to sort out and classify it.

'The Count of Montenegro's rooms are decorated with antique marbles and bronzes which come from either the excavations at Aricia or were bought in Rome by the Cardinal. One also sees many paintings of the Spanish and Italian Schools, some of which would not be out of place in the finest galleries of Europe.'

I must say something about Belver, or Bellver Castle, the ancient residence of the Majorcan Kings. I have only seen it from afar, majestically dominating the sea from the top of a hill. This is a very ancient fortress, and one of the harshest state prisons in Spain.

'The existing and well preserved walls,' writes M. Laurens, 'were raised towards the end of the thirteenth century; and it is one of the most fascinatingly interesting examples of mediaeval architecture in existence today.'

When our traveller[15] visited the Castle, as I did not, he found some fifty Carlist prisoners, ragged and almost naked, some still

---

[15] M. Laurens *(Translator's note.)*

almost children, cheerfully filling their mess-tins from a cauldron of coarsely boiled macaroni. They were guarded by soldiers who, with cigars hanging from their mouths, were knitting stockings.

In fact, it was during this period that the overflow from the prisons of Barcelona had been diverted to the Castle of Belver. But more celebrated prisoners saw these formidable doors close behind them.

It was here, imprisoned in the dungeon of the *'torre de homenage, cuya cuva es la más cruda prisón.'* (the 'Tower of Homage,' writes Vargas, 'which is the most crude of prisons.') that Don Gaspar de Jovellanos, one of the most eloquent orators and compelling writers of Spain, atoned for the sin of having written his famous pamphlet *Bread and Bulls*. He spent his cheerless leisure making a precise description of the Castle, revoking many of the tragic events that it had witnessed during the Mediaeval wars.

Due to his enforced stay on the island, the Majorcans have a superb description of their Cathedral and their Exchange. In a word, his *Letters on Majorca* are the most reliable source of information available that one can consult.

The same dungeon which Jovellanos occupied during the parasitic reign of the Prince of Peace, very soon received another scientific and political celebrity.

This is the little known story of a man equally famous in France as Jovellanos is in Spain. It is of great interest because it is one romantic chapter in a life in which the love of science is precipitated into thousands of hazardous and stirring adventures.

Castle of Bellver. (J. B. Laurens, 1839).

Chapter III

M. ARAGO, who had been commissioned by Napoleon to measure the meridian, was, in 1808, working in Majorca on a mountain called *Clot de Galatzo*, when news was received of events at Madrid and the abduction of Ferdinand.[16] The indignation of the inhabitants of Majorca was so great, that they set out for the mountain, to seize and kill the French scientist.

This mountain rises above the coast where James I first landed before conquering Majorca from the Moors; and as Arago often used to light fires for his own use, they decided that he was signalling a French squadron with a landing force.

Damian, an islander and quartermaster of the Spanish naval brig assigned by the Spanish government to assist in the operation of measuring the meridian, resolved to warn M. Arago of the danger he was in. Running ahead of his compatriots, he managed to give the scientist some sailor clothes to disguise himself.

M. Arago immediately left the mountain and hastened towards Palma. On the way, he met with those who were on their way to tear him to pieces; they asked him for information of the accursed *gabacho*, whom they wished to get rid of. Being

---

[16] King Ferdinand VII. *(Translator's note.)*

perfectly fluent in the language of the country, he was able to answer all their questions without being recognized.

Arriving in Palma he boarded the brig; but Captain Manuel de Vacaro, who had until then always obeyed his orders, refused to take him to Barcelona, and the only refuge he offered on board was a crate which proved too small for M. Arago to get into.

The next day a threatening mob gathered on the waterfront and Captain Vacaro warned M. Arago that he could no longer answer for his life; adding, on the advice of the Captain-General, that his only hope of safety lay in imprisonment in the Castle of Belver. He was provided with a launch to cross the bay. The mob spotted him and gave chase, and were almost on him as the doors of fortress closed behind him.

He spent two months in this prison until at last the Captain-General advised him that he would turn a blind eye to his escape, which he made good with the aid of M. Rodríguez, his Spanish associate in the measuring of the meridian.

The same Damian, the Majorcan who saved his life at the Clot de Galatzo, took him by fishing boat to Algiers, but would not, for any price, land him either in France or in Spain.

During his captivity, M. Arago had been informed by his Swiss guards that certain monks of the island had promised them money if they poisoned him.

In Africa, our scientist met with many other setbacks, from which he miraculously managed to escape; but this has nothing to do with our topic, and we hope that he will one day publish this fascinating story.

At first sight, the Majorcan capital does not reveal its character. Only by roaming its core, and penetrating its deep and mysterious streets at dusk, can one appreciate the graceful style and original placing of even its less important buildings; but its African aspect is most apparent when approaching Palma from the northern inland fields.

M. Laurens sensed this picturesque beauty, something that would not have struck an ordinary archeologist. He has described a view which overwhelmed me with its melancholy and its grandeur; a section of the city wall, not far from the Church of St. Augustin, where a huge square block rises, with no opening other than a small arched door.

This structure, the last vestige of a Templar fortress, is crowned by a cluster of beautiful palm-trees, forming a poignant foreground, splendid in its bareness, for the magnificent panorama that unfolded from the foot of the wall with the prosperous and fertile plain that stretched to the distant blue mountains of Valldemosa. Towards evening the colours of the landscape change by the hour, becoming ever more harmonious; at sunset we have watched it change from a sparkling pink to a magnificent purple, then to a silvery lilac, and ultimately, at onset of night, to a pure transparent blue.

M. Laurens has drawn many other views from the ramparts of Palma.

'Every evening,' he writes, 'at the hour when the sun coloured things most vividly, I strolled slowly along the ramparts, stopping at each step to gaze at the fortuitous harmony produced by the relationship of the outline of the mountains or the sea with the silhouette of the city buildings.

'Here the embankments on the inner side of the ramparts were covered with a frightful hedge of aloes, from which sprang hundreds of tall flowering stalks resembling an enormous candelabra. In the gardens beyond, clumps of palm trees grow midst fig-trees, cacti, orange-trees and castor-oil plants as tall as trees; farther off, belvederes and vines shaded the terraces; and finally the Cathedral spires, the bell-towers and domes of the many churches stood silhouetted against the pure and luminous background of the sky.'

Another walk in which M. Laurens's preferences concurred with mine was that between the ruins of the Dominican Monastery.

At the end of a vine arbour supported by marble columns, were four tall palm-trees which seemed gigantic because of the elevation of their terrace-garden. From this vantage point, they formed an integral part of the city skyline. Through their fronds one caught sight of the top of the façade of St. Etienne, the massive tower holding the famous Balearic clock[17] and the Angel Tower of the Royal Palace.

This monastery of the Inquisition which is now a mere heap of debris, where some scruffy trees and a few aromatic plants thrive in the rubble, did not fall by the hand of time. Only a few years ago a swifter and more inexorable hand, that of the revolution, destroyed and reduced to dust what is said to have been an architectural masterpiece; and so its remnants, fragments of rich mosaic, skeletons of some delicate arches, still standing in a void, bear witness to its past glory.

The destruction throughout Spain of these sanctuaries of Catholic art is still a subject of great indignation among the Palma aristocracy, and a source of genuine regret among artists. Ten years ago, I too might have been more struck by the van-

---

[17] This clock, already described in detail by two of the most important Majorcan historians, Dameto and Mut, was still functioning thirty years ago. M. Grasset de Saint-Sauveur writes: "This very ancient piece of machinery is known as the *Sun Clock*. It marks the hours from sunrise to sunset, more or less following the greater or lesser extension of the diurnal and nocturnal arc; with the result that, on the 10th of June, it strikes the first hour of the day at half-past five, and the fourteenth at half-past seven, the first of the night at half past eight, the ninth at half past four the next morning. Beginning with December 10th, the process is reversed. Throughout the year the hours are accurately regulated by the variations between sunrise and sunset. This clock is of no great use to the people, who use modern clocks, but it serves the gardeners by reminding them of their watering-hours. No one knows from where and when this mechanism was brought to Palma; it most probably did not come from Spain, France, Germany or Italy, where the Romans had introduced the practice of dividing the day into twelve hours, beginning with sunrise.

"However, an ecclesiastic, Rector of the University of Palma, assures us in the third part of his work on the Seraphic religion that, under Vespasian, Jewish refugees rescued this famous clock from the ruins of Jerusalem and carried it to Majorca, where they fled for safety. So here is a really wonderful origin that is really in keeping with islanders characteristic fondness for all that savours of the miraculous.

"The historian Dameto, and his successor Mut, trace the Balearic Clock back only to the year 1385, claiming that it was bought from the Dominican Fathers and set in the tower were it still exists."

(Journey to the Balearic and Pityusian Isles (1807).

dalism of this destruction than by the page of history which it illustrates.

Yet though there is good reason to deplore - as M. Marliani does in his *Political History of Modern Spain* - the weak and at the same time violent side of the measures which this decree was to entail, I must confess that standing among these ruins I felt an emotion which was not the sorrow they usually inspired. Lightning had struck there, and lightning is a blind instrument, a force as brutal as the fury of man; but the law of Providence that governs the elements and presides over its apparent confusion, well knows that the beginnings of a new life lies hidden under the ashes of its ruins. On the day the monasteries fell, one could sense in the political atmosphere of Spain something analogous to a need for renewal which Nature experiences in her fruitful convulsions.

I could not believe, when I was told in Palma, that this act of violence was carried out by a few malcontents, greedy for revenge or booty, before the eyes of the horrified people. A great number of malcontents would have been needed to reduce a building of such proportions to dust, and only a people with very little feeling would stand and watch the implementation of a decree that genuinely offended them.

I would rather believe that the first stone thrown from the top of these domes tore from the soul of the people a feeling of fear and respect no more firmly established there than the monastic bell-tower had been on its foundations; and that each one, deep down inside, felt stirred by a strange and sudden urge, and hurled themselves onto the corpse with a mixture of courage and fear, fury and remorse. The monastic system sheltered many malpractices and greatly fostered egoism; religion is very powerful in Spain, and no doubt more than one demolisher repented and confessed to the monk whom he had just chased from his sanctuary. But in the heart of the most ignorant and most blind man something makes him quiver with enthusiasm when destiny confers a sovereign mission upon him.

With their money and their sweat the Spanish people had built these haughty palaces of the regular clergy, to whose doors they came, century after century, to receive the farthing of idle beggardom and the bread of intellectual bondage. They had participated with the clergy in their crimes and shown equal cowardice. They had helped them pile the stakes of the Inquisition. They had been accessories and informers in the atrocious persecutions of whole races which they wished to root out from their midst. And once they achieved the ruin of the Jews who had enriched them, and had expelled the Moors to whom they owed their civilization and greatness, they were chastised by Heaven with poverty and ignorance. They had enough perseverance and piety not to blame the clergy, and suffered a long time under this yoke made by their own hands. Nevertheless, they one day heard strange, bold voices addressing their ears and consciousness with words of liberation and freedom. They, realizing the errors of their forefathers, blushed at their humiliation, felt outraged by their poverty, and despite their continued idolatrous attitude towards images and relics, smashed these and believed more fiercely in their rights than in their creed.

What, then, is this secret power which suddenly transforms the fanaticism of the devote and prostrate against the objects of his lifelong worship? It is certainly neither discontentment with other people, nor boredom with things. It is dissatisfaction with oneself, the apathy of one's own weakness.

And the Spanish people were greater on that day than is generally known. They performed a decisive deed and denied themselves the slightest possibility of returning to their original convictions, like a child who wants to be a man and breaks all his toys, so as not to be tempted by them again.

Don Juan Mendizabal (whose name well deserves a mention in this context), and if what I have heard of his political career is reliable, was more a man of principles rather than of action. In my opinion this statesman over-rated the intellectual capacity of Spain at one period, and under-rated it at another, for on some occasion he took untimely or inadequate measures, sowing his ideas on barren fields where the seed was choked or devoured, is perhaps sufficient reason for which he was denied the practical ability and inflexible nature needed for the immediate success of such undertakings; but there is no reason why history, looked upon from a more philosophical point of view than is usual, should not one day hail him as one of the most generous and most enthusiastically progressive minds of Spain.[18]

I often thought about this among the ruins of the Majorcan monasteries, for when we heard his name being cursed, it would have been awkward for us to defend him with honour and sympathy. I told myself that, excluding the political issues of the day, which I may be well permitted to profess I have neither a liking nor the aptitude for, I could at least form a synthetic judgement on men and on events, without fear of becoming ridiculous. It is not nearly so necessary, as some believe and insist, to have direct knowledge of a nation, and to make exhaustive studies of its customs and material conditions, in order to have

---

[18] M. Marliani's honesty and his great feeling for history inspired him to utter the following tribute, while criticizing M. Mendizábal's government: "One will never be able to deny him these qualities, all the more admirable for having been seldom encountered among his predecessors in office: this living faith in the future of the country, this boundless devotion to the cause of freedom, this passionate sense of patriotism, and this genuine enthusiasm for progressive and even revolutionary ideas that could bring about reforms so needed in Spain; this great tolerance and generosity towards his enemies; this lack of personal ambition, which at all times and in all circumstances made him sacrifice his own interests to those of Spain, left him, on leaving the many ministries, without a single ribbon in his lapel... He was the first minister to take the regeneration of his country seriously. His term in office marked real progress. He was a minister who spoke with the voice of a patriot. He did not have the power to abolish censorship, but he generously freed the Press of its fetters, to the advantage of his enemies. He submitted his administrative actions to the free review of public opinion; and when he was violently opposed (instigated by some of his former friends) in Parliament, he had the tremendous dignity to respect the rights of a certain deputy while the latter was acting in his official capacity. He told the Tribune that he would rather cut off his hand than sign an order for dismissal of this deputy, whom he had loaded with honours, but who had since become his most bitter political opponent. This noble example given by M. Mendizábal deserves greater praise in that such conduct was wholly unprecedented and has since found no imitators. After him there has been no one to equal this quality of tolerance." (*Histoire politique de l'Espagne moderne,* par M. Marliani)

a clear idea and a real understanding of its history, its future, and in a word, its spiritual character. It seems to me that in the general history of human life there is one main line to follow, which is the same in every nation, and to which the threads of each private history are attached. This line is the longing for and the perpetual striving towards the Ideal, or, if you wish, the perfectibility, which man has always carried within himself, whether in the form of blind instinct or dazzling theory. Truly eminent men have all been aware of this and practised it in some way or the other, but the most bold, those to whom the vision was most clearly revealed, have struck the most daring blows in the present to hasten the course of the future, are those who are almost always misjudged by their contemporaries. They have been misunderstood, slandered and condemned, and only when the fruit of their labour has been harvested are they replaced on their pedestals from which they had been toppled by some transient disappointments and a few unexplained setbacks.

How many famous Revolutionary leaders have been belatedly and hesitantly restored to fame! And how little understood and undeveloped their missionary work still remains! In Spain, Mendizábal was one of the most harshly judged ministers, yet he was the most courageous of them all, perhaps the only courageous one; and the unforgettable deed which marked his short term in office, the complete destruction of the monasteries, for which he has been so severely reproached that I feel the need to cite in his defence the determination and zeal with which the Spanish people agreed to carry it out.

This, at least, is the feeling that suddenly overwhelmed my soul while viewing these ruins, not yet blackened by time and which also seemed to protest against the past and proclaim the awakening of truth in the hearts of the people. I do not believe that I have lost my taste and respect for the arts, and I do not feel I harbour instincts of vengeance and barbarity, finally, I am not one of those who claim beauty is useless and that our historic monuments should be turned into factories; but a monastery of the Inquisition razed to the ground by the hands of the people is a page of history no less great, no less instructive, and no less stirring than a Roman aqueduct or amphitheatre. A governmental order, based on paltry utility or absurd economy, which commands the cold blooded destruction of such a Temple would be a lamentable and criminal act; but a political leader who, on a day of crisis and danger, sacrifices art and science to the more precious considerations of reason, justice and religious freedom, and a people who despite their religious instincts, their love of Catholic pomp and their reverence for monks, find sufficient strength of heart and power to execute this decree at a moment's notice, are like the crew of a storm-tossed boat who jettison their valuables in order to save their lives.

Weep then who will, over the ruins! Nearly all the buildings whose downfall we deplore were dungeons where for centuries the bodies and spirits of men had languished. And may poets come who, rather than mourn the passing of the world's infancy, will acclaim in their verse, over fragments of gilded baubles and blood-stained rods, its manly coming of age. There are some beautiful lines written by Chamisso on his ancestral chateau which had been destroyed in the French Revolution. The poem ends with a thought as novel in poetry as in politics:

"Blessed are you, ancient manor, over whom now the plough-share drives!

And blessed is he who drives the plough-share over you"

Having evoked the memory of this beautiful poem, dare I transcribe a few pages of prose inspired by my visit to a Dominican monastery? Why not, for why should the reader not show some indulgence, when asked to pass judgement on a thought which the authoress has sacrificed her self-esteem and her deep-seated tendencies to create? May this fragment, for what it is worth, cast a little variety into the dry catalogue of buildings I have been describing!

Chapter IV
The Monastery of the Inquisition

Two men met by the calm light of the moon in the ruins of a monastery. One appeared to be in the prime of life, the other, although bent beneath the weight of years, was the younger of the two.

Both trembled on meeting one another, for it was late at night, the road was deserted and the Cathedral clock slowly and mournfully tolled the hour.

The apparently older one spoke first.

'Whoever you may be, my man,' he said, 'you have nothing to fear from me; I am weak and broken. You can take nothing from me, for I am poor and destitute.'

'Friend,' replied the young man, 'I am only hostile to those who attack me, and, like you, I am too poor to fear robbers,'

'Brother,' answered the man with the haggard features, 'why did you start when I approached you?'

'Because, like all artists, I am somewhat superstitious, and took you for the ghost of one of the monks who are no longer here and whose graves we are now treading. And you, friend, why were you frightened at my approach?'

'Because, like all monks, being very superstitious, I took you for the ghost of one of those monks who once buried me alive in one of the graves beneath your feet.'

'What are you saying? Are you one of those men for whom I have eagerly and unavailingly searched for all over Spain?'

'You will no longer find us anywhere under the light of the sun; but in the shadows of the night you may still come upon us. Now that your wish is granted, what do you want with a monk?'

'To look at you, to question you, father; to engrave your features in memory to reproduce them on canvas. I want to gather up your words and repeat them to my fellow citizens. I want to get to know you so that I may be able to imbibe the mystery, the poetry and the greatness ingrained in the person of a monk and of life in a monastery.'

'Where do you get these strange ideas, traveller? Do you not come from a land where Papal rule has been rejected, the monks banished and the monasteries suppressed?'

'There are still among us those devoted souls who revere the past, and whose fervent imaginations are struck by the poetry of the Middle Ages. We seek, we venerate and we almost worship all that can bring us the faintest fragrance of this past. Ah, Father, do not believe that we are all blind desecrators. We artists abhor the savages who defile and break all they touch. Far from approving their decrees of death and destruction, we endeavour in our paintings, in our poems, in our theatres, and in all our other works to revive ancient traditions and to reanimate the spirit of mysticism which that sublime child, Christian Art has engendered.'

'What are you saying, my son? Is it possible that the artists of your free and prosperous country are finding inspiration elsewhere than in the present? They have so many new things to sing, to paint and to illustrate, how can they live, as you say, bowed over the graves of their ancestors? How can they search in the dust of the tombs for lively, fruitful inspiration, when God, in His goodness, has given them a sweet and gracious life?'

'Good monk, I do not know if our way of life is as you picture it. We artists do not bother with politics, and social question interest us even less. We would look in vain for poetry in our surroundings. The arts are languishing, inspiration is smothered, bad taste triumphs, material needs absorb man; and if we could not worship the past and if we did not have the monuments of past centuries to fortify us, the sacred fire which we struggle to keep alive would soon be extinguished.'

'Nevertheless, I have been told that human genius has never made such progress as in the art of good living, the marvels of industry and the blessings of freedom. Am I mistaken?'

'If you were told, Father, that in no former time had such opulence and comfort been obtained from material riches, or that from the collapse of pre-Revolutionary society such a frightening diversity of tastes, opinions and beliefs would emerge, that was the truth. But if you were not told that all these things, instead of making us happy, have merely debased and corrupted us, you were not told the whole truth.'

'But from where does this strange result come? How come that all sources of happiness become poison on your lips, and that the well-being and freedom and that which makes man great, just and good, have made you mean and miserable? Can you explain this paradox?'

'Father, do I have to remind you that man does not live by bread alone? Since we have lost our faith, none of that which we have acquired is of benefit to our souls.'

'My son, explain to me then, how is it that you have lost your faith when religious persecutions have ceased and you are able to expand your souls and raise your eyes to the divine light? That was the moment of belief, for it was the moment of knowledge. And yet, at that moment you doubted? What clouded your minds?'

'The cloud of human weakness and anguish. Surely investigation is not compatible with faith, Father?'

'Young man, it is as if you asked me whether faith is incompatible with truth. Do you not believe in anything, my son? Or do you believe in falsehood?'

'Alas, I believe only in Art. But is that not enough to uplift the soul with strength, confidence and sublime joy?'

'I do not know, my son, and I do not yet understand. Are any of you people still happy? And you, have you managed to avoid depression and sorrow?'

'No, Father; artists are the most unhappy, the most angry and most tormented of men, for each day they see the thing they venerate fall a little lower and all their efforts to uplift it, are in vain.'

'But how is it that men, imbued with such a conviction as yours, can allow the arts to perish instead of revitalizing it.'

'It is because we lack faith, and without faith art cannot flourish.'

'But have you not told me that Art is your religion? You are contradicting yourself, or perhaps it is that I have not understood you.'

'But how can we not contradict ourselves, Father! We, to whom God has given a mission which the world denies us, we, for whom the present closes the doors of glory, inspiration and life; we, who are forced to live in the past, to question the dead about the secrets of eternal beauty which man today has forgotten how to worship and overturned their altars? Standing before great masterpieces, we are filled with vigour and enthusiasm as well as the hope of being able to equal them; but when we attempt to realize our ambitious dreams, a cold wind of disdain and ridicule blows on us from a bigoted and doubting world, and we are unable to produce anything worthy of our ideal, and thoughts wither in our bosom before they are born.'

The young artist spoke with bitterness, the moon illuminating his proud young face, while the motionless monk gazed gently upon him in surprise.

'Let us sit here,' said the latter after a moment of silence, pausing beside the solid balustrade of a terrace that overlooked the city, countryside and the sea.

It was in a corner of the Dominicans' garden which had previously been filled with flowers, fountains and precious marbles, but was now scattered with debris and overrun by tall weeds which grow with such vigour and speed among ruins.

The Traveller, in his excitement, crushed one of these in his hand and threw it away with a cry of pain. The monk smiled.

'That prick is sharp,' he said, 'but not dangerous. My son, that bramble which you so carelessly grasp and which wounds you is symbolic of the boorish men of whom you were just complaining. They infest palaces and monasteries. They overrun the altars and install themselves on the debris of ancient splendours of this world. Look with what verve and tenacity these weeds have invaded the flower-beds where we grew with such care the delicate and precious plants of which none survive. Thus the simple and half-savage men, who were thrown out like the useless weeds have reclaimed their rights, to smother the poisonous plant which grew in the shade known as the Inquisition.'

'Why could they not have smothered it without destroying the sanctuaries of Christian art and the works of genius?'

'They had to tear that cursed plant out by the roots, because it was vigorous and widespread. They even had to destroy the very foundations of these cloisters where the roots were hidden.'

'But, Father, these thorny weeds which have taken over, of what beauty or use are they?'

The monk paused for an instant and replied:

'You told me that you are a painter, and without doubt you will sketch these ruins?'

'Certainly. But why do you ask me?'

'Will you, then, leave out from your drawing those huge brambles, falling in festoons over the rubble, and swaying in the wind, or will you use them as a fitting detail in your composition, as I have once seen in a painting by Salvator Rosa?'

'They are an inseparable accessory of the ruins, and no painter could fail to make use of them.'

'Therefore, they have their beauty, their significance and consequently, their use?'

'Your parable is not very just, Father. Put beggars and gypsies among these ruins and it would become more sinister and desolate. The painting would gain, but what would humanity gain?'

'Yes, perhaps a better painting, and certainly a very good lesson. Yet you artists, who provide this lesson, are unaware of what you are doing, and see nothing here but fallen stones and growing grass.'

'You are hard on me; from what you say, I could well reply that you saw nothing in this catastrophe other than the destruction of your prison and the recovery of your freedom; for I suspect, Father, that the monastery was by no means to your liking.'

'And you, my son, would you have carried your love of art and poetry to the extent of living here without regret?'

'I imagine it as the most beautiful life in the world. Oh, what a vast monastery of noble style this must have been. How these ruins proclaim its former splendour and elegance! How pleasant it must have been to come here of an evening, to breathe in the sweet breeze and dream to the sound of the sea, when these airy galleries were paved with rich mosaics, when crystalline waters murmured in marble pools, and a silver lamp, like a pale star, shone out of the depths of the monastery! What profound peace, what exalted silence you must have enjoyed when the respect and confidence of your people surrounded you with an impregnable wall, when they crossed themselves and lowered their voices each time they passed before your mysterious portals! Oh, who would not gladly renounce all the cares, anxieties and ambitions of social life if he might come and bury himself here in tranquil oblivion of the whole world, remaining an artist and to be able to devote ten, perhaps twenty, years to a single painting, which he would polish slowly like a precious diamond, and which he would see set upon an altar, not to be judged and criticized by every ignoramus, but to be revered and acknowledged as an image worthy of the Deity itself.'

'Stranger,' the monk replied severely, 'your words are filled with pride and your dreams are vain indeed! In this art of which you speak so pompously, and which you extol so highly, you see only yourself, and the isolation for which you yearn would be no more to you than a means of self-aggrandisement and deification. I now understand how you can believe in this selfish Art without any religious faith or social sense. But perhaps you have not allowed these thoughts to mature before speaking; perhaps you are unaware of what took place in these dens of corruption and terror. Come with me, and perhaps what I am going to show you will change your feelings and your thoughts.'

The monk led the young traveller, not without danger, across mounds of loose rubble to the centre of the ruined monastery; and there, where the prisons had been, he carefully made him descend along the side of a solid mass of masonry about fifteen feet thick, which had been split open to its depths by pickaxe and shovel. At the core of this terrifying crust of stone and cement, like gaping jaws in the bowels of the earth, small cells appeared, airless and without light and separated from one another by blocks of masonry as thick as the keystones of their gloomy vaults.

'Young man,' said the monk, 'these pits are not wells, nor even graves; they are the dungeons of the Inquisition. It is here, over the centuries, that those who dared think differently to the Inquisition, whether they were guilty or innocent in the eyes of God, whether they were depraved by vice or tormented by passion, died a slow death.

'These Dominican fathers were scholars, men of letters, even artists. In their vast libraries the refinements of theology, bound in gilt and morroco leather volumes, edged with pearls and rubies, were displayed on ebony shelves; yet man, that living book in which God Himself had recorded his thoughts, had been interred to an isolated existence in the bowels of the earth. They owned vessels of chased silver, chalices glittering with priceless stones, magnificent paintings, gold and ivory Madonnas;

and yet Man, that chosen vessel, that chalice filled with heavenly grace, that living image of God, they delivered him alive to the chill of death and the worms of the tomb! Some cultivated roses and jonquils with as much love and care as a mother bestows on her child, yet they felt no pity when they saw their fellow-man, their brother, grown pale and mouldering in the damp tomb.

'That, my son, is what monks and monasteries are about! Brutal ferocity on the one side, shameful cowardice on the other; selfish intelligence with a merciless piety, that was the Inquisition.

'And if, while opening these squalid pits to light of Heaven, the hand of the liberators knocked down some columns or defaced some gilding, must the slab be replaced over the tomb of the dying victims, and must we bemoan the fate of their executioners now deprived of gold and slaves?'

The artist had descended into one of the cells to examine with curiosity one of its walls. For a moment he tried to imagine the struggle which the human mind, buried alive, could sustain against the frightful despair of such a captivity. But no sooner had he painted this picture in his impressionable imagination, he was filled with anxiety and terror. He believed he felt those icy vaults pressing down on his soul; his limbs trembled and he was unable to breathe, he felt faint as he tried to leap out of the abyss and he cried out as he stretched his arms to the monk:

'Help me, Father, in the name of Heaven, help me get out of here!'

'Well, my son,' said the monk, stretching out his hand to him, 'if you are relieved at the sight of the stars shining overhead, imagine how I felt when I saw the sun again after ten years of similar torment.'

'Unhappy monk!' cried the traveller, hastening back towards the garden, 'How could you endure ten years of anticipated death without loosing your reason or your life? Had I stayed there a moment longer, I certainly would have become an idiot or a madman. No, I could never have thought that the sight of a dungeon would arouse such sudden and profound terror in me, and I don't understand how the mind can grow accustomed and submit to such a fate! I have seen the instruments of torture in Venice; I have also seen the dungeons of the Ducal Palace, the sombre blind alley where victims fell, struck by an unseen hand, and the perforated flagstone through which their blood dripped into the canal below, leaving no trace; this left me with the impression of a more or less swift death. But that dungeon into which I have just descended, it is the appalling idea of life that horrifies the mind. Oh, God! To be there and unable to die!'

'Look at me, my son,' said the monk, uncovering his bald and wrinkled head. 'I have lived not much more than you, you with your virile face and untroubled brow, and yet, without doubt, you must have taken me for an old man.

'What I did to deserve my slow torment, and how I endured it, is of little importance. I do not ask for your pity; I no longer need it, for I feel happy and young at the sight of these toppled walls and the empty dungeons. Nor do I not wish to inspire in you a horror of the monks; they are now free, and so am I, God is good to all. But, because you are an artist, you will have bene-fited by experiencing an emotion without which the artist is unable to understand his work.

'If you were now to paint these ruins where you wished to weep for the past, and where I come every night to prostrate myself and give thanks to God for the present, perhaps your hand and your genius would be inspired by loftier feelings than faint-hearted regret or sterile admiration. As far as the monu-ments are concerned, though of incalculable value to antiqua-rians, they have no other merit than that of recalling the deeds which humanity consecrated by their erection, and these were often iniquitous or puerile. Since you have travelled, you may have seen in Genoa a bridge, with enormous piers, crossing a deep chasm, built by a conceited patrician. On the other side stands a graceless and costly church which he erected in an uninhabited district because he was too vain either to cross the stream to worship elsewhere or to kneel beside the members of his parish. You may have also seen the Egyptian pyramids, a hideous testimony to the slavery of nations; or the dolmens, over which torrents of human blood flowed to slake the unquenchable thirst of barbaric gods. But most of you artists see only the beautiful or the singularity of execution in the works on man, and are impervious to the ideas that this work substantiates. Consequently your intellect often worships an emotion which your heart, if it had a conscience, would reject.

'That is why your own works very often lack the true colour of life, especially when, instead of portraying that which circulates through the veins of humanity, you coldly force yourselves to portray the dead which you have no wish to understand.'

'Father,' replied the young man, 'I understand what you mean and I do not entirely reject your lesson; but do you believe that Art can draw inspiration from such a philosophy? You expound, with the reasoning of today, a doctrine which was conceived in a poetic frenzy by the ingenious superstition of our fathers. If, instead of the smiling deities of Greece, we were to lay bare the commonplace allegories concealed beneath their voluptuous forms; if, instead of the divine Madonna of the Florentine School, we were to paint, like the Dutch, a sturdy bar-maid; and finally, if we turned Jesus, the Son of God, into a naïve Platonic philosopher, we would be left with man instead of a Godhead; just as here, instead of a Christian church, we look upon a pile of shattered stones.'

'My son,' replied the monk, 'if the Florentines gave the Virgin divine features, it was because they still believed in her; and if the Dutch gave her common features, that was because they no longer believed in her. And you artists, you who today only believe in Art, and you who boast of painting sacred pictures, you will never succeed. Do not try to return to the past, paint what is unmistakably alive and of the present day.

'Had I been an artist, I should have devoted a painting to the day of my liberation: I would have painted bold sturdy men with hammers in one hand and torches in the other, breaking into this limbo which I have just shown you, and ghosts with dulled eyes and fearful smiles would be rising from the fetid flagstones. I should have shown a heavenly light falling on my rescuers through the cracked vaults, forming a halo about their heads. This would have been a marvellous subject, well-suited to my times, as Michelangelos's Last Judgement was to his; for these men, who appear to you nothing more than coarse and brutal vandals, seemed to me more noble and more glorious than all the angels of Heaven. This very ruin, which for you is an object of sadness and distress, has become for me a monument more sacred than it ever was before its fall.

'If I were entrusted with raising an altar that should bear witness to future generations of the greatness and power of our generation, I should ask for nothing better than this mound of rubble, above which I should set a consecrated stone with this inscription:

"Here, on this altar, and in the days of ignorance and cruelty, men worshipped a God of revenge and torture. On the Day of Justice, and in the name of Humanity, men overturned these bloodstained altars, abominable to the God of Mercy!" '

*The Tower of the Cathedral of Palma seen from the ruins of the
Convent of St. Domingo. (Drawing by F. X. Parcerisa, 1842).*

Chapter V

IT was not in Palma, but among the ruins of the House of the Inquisition in Barcelona that I saw those dungeons which had been enclosed in solid blocks of masonry fourteen feet thick. It is very possible that when the people of Palma broke open the dungeons there were no prisoners. It is only proper that I must apologize to the susceptible Majorcans for the poetic licence I have taken in the previous chapter.

However, there is no invention without a certain basis of truth, and I may mention that I met a priest in Majorca, now the rector of a parish in Palma, who told me he had spent seven years of his life, the flower of his youth, in the prisons of the Inquisition, and he was released only through the intervention of a lady who held him in respect. He was a man in the prime of life, with bright eyes and a happy disposition. He did not appear to regret very much the passing of the regime of the Holy Office.

Let me quote a passage from Grasset de Sainte-Sauveur regarding this Dominican monastery, which is plainly unbiased, for in the introduction he writes a flattering eulogy of the Majorcan Inquisitors whom he had met:

"...However, one can still see, in the cloisters of St. Dominic, paintings which record the barbaric atrocities committed against the Jews. Each of the unfortunate victims who was burned at the stake is represented, and written at the base of the picture are his name, age and the date of his execution.

"I was assured that a few years ago the descendants of these hapless men, who today form a separate class among the inhabitants of Palma, under the ridiculous name of *'chouettes'* (screech-owls), had unsuccessfully offered great sums to have these distressing records obliterated. I find this difficult to believe.

"Yet I shall never forget how one day, while strolling through the Dominican cloisters and sorrowfully examining those sad pictures, a monk approached me and pointing out that several of them were marked with a skull and cross bones said: 'These are portraits of those whose ashes were exhumed and thrown to the winds.'

"My blood froze and I left abruptly, broken hearted and stricken to the soul.

"By chance I came across a report printed in 1755, by order of the Inquisition. It contained the names, surnames, occupations and offences of all those unfortunates who had been sentenced in Majorca between the years 1645 and 1691.

"I shuddered as I read this document: I found that four Majorcans, one a woman, had been burned alive for Judaism; in the dungeons of the Inquisition thirty-two others had died for the same offence, and their bodies then burned; in three cases the ashes were exhumed and thrown to the winds; a Dutchman charged with Lutheranism; a Majorcan charged with Mohammedanism; six Portuguese, one a woman, and seven Majorcans charged with Judaism; were all burned in effigy, having had the good fortune to escape. In all, I counted two hundred and sixteen other victims, Majorcans and foreigners, charged with Judaism, heresy or Mohammedanism, who were released from prison after having publicly recanted and returned to the bosom of the Church."

This ghastly catalogue wound up with a no less shocking decree of the Inquisition:"All the offenders listed in this report have been publicly condemned by the Holy Office, as avowed heretics; all their possessions have been confiscated and handed over to the Royal Treasury; they have been declared incompetent and disqualified from holding or acceding to any rank or benefices, whether ecclesiastical or secular, or any other public offices or honours; they are debarred from wearing on their persons, or allowing to be worn by their dependants, gold, silver, pearls, precious stones, coral, silk, camlet, or broadcloth; or riding on horseback, carrying arms, or practising and using the other things which, by common law, the laws and pragmatic sanctions of this Kingdom, or the directions and style of the Holy Office, are prohibited to persons thus degraded; the same prohibition is extended, in the case of women under sentence of burning, to their sons and daughters, and in the case of men, down to their grandchildren on the male line; at the same time condemning the memory of those executed in effigy, ordaining that their bones (provided that these can de distinguished from those of faithful Christians) shall be exhumed, handed over to justice and to the secular arm, to be burned and reduced to ashes; likewise, all inscriptions or coats of arms that appear on their tombs, wherever they may be, whether affixed, or painted shall be obliterated or scraped away, *so that nothing of them remains on this earth, except the memory of their sentence and their execution."*

When one reads a recent document such as this, and when one observes the unyielding hatred by which, even after twelve to fifteen generations of conversion to Christianity, the unhappy Jews are still pursued in Majorca, it is hard to believe that the spirit of the Inquisition had been totally extinguished there as was said at the time of Mendizábal's decree.

I shall not close this chapter nor leave the convent of the Inquisition without disclosing to my readers a rather curious discovery, the whole credit for which belongs to M. Tastu, and which would have made that scholars' fortune some thirty years ago, unless he had taken it, light-heartedly and without any thought of reimbursement, to the Master of the World, which is probably what he would have done because, like all true artists, he had a carefree and easy-going nature.

This note is far too interesting to be curtailed. Here it is, exactly as it was placed in my hands, with permission to publish it.

'The Monastery of St. Dominic in Palma, Majorca

'Miguel de Fabra, a friend of St. Dominic, founded the Order of Preaching Friars in Majorca. He came from Old Castile, and he accompanied James I in 1229 in the conquest of the Greater Balearic Island. His knowledge was profound and varied, and his piety remarkable; which gave him some authority over the Conqueror, his nobles who accompanied him and even the ordinary soldiers. He not only addressed the troops, celebrated the divine Mass and dispensed Holy Communion, but he also fought against the infidels as was then the custom of the clergy. The Moors claimed that the Holy Virgin and Father Miguel alone had conquered them. It was said that the Aragonese and Catalan soldiers addressed their prayers, after God and the Blessed Virgin, to Father Miguel Fabra.

'This illustrious Dominican had received the habit of his order in Toulouse from the hands of his friend Dominic: he was sent by him to Paris with two others on an important mission. It was he who established the first Dominican monastery in Palma, with the help of a donation made to him by the Bursar of the first Bishop of Majorca, Don J. R. de Torella; this was in the year 1231.

'A mosque and a few measures of land belonging to it, were used for the first foundation. Later, the preaching friars enlarged their community by means of a profitable trade in all kinds of commodities, as well as by the frequent donations of their faithful. However, Miguel de Fabra's brother had gone to die in Valencia, which he had helped to conquer.

'Jaime Fabra was the architect of the Dominican convent. He is not said to have been related to Father Miguel, his namesake; he is known to have handed in his plans about the year 1296, and that he later drafted those of the Cathedral of Barcelona (1317) and several others in the kingdom of Aragon.

'It is apparent, when examining the different features of the ruined building, as we have done, that the monastery and its church must have undergone many changes in the course of time. Here are the shaky remains of a sumptuous door in the style of the fourteenth century; but further on, and still forming part of the building, are shattered arches and weighty keystones lying on the rubble, demonstrating the work of other architects considerably inferior to Jaime Fabra.

'Over these vast ruins, where nothing but some ancient palm-trees remain, preserved at our urgent plea, we were able to lament, as we did over the ruins of the Convent of Santa Catalina in Barcelona, that the cold and passionless hand of politics brought about these undiscriminating acts of destruction.

'As a matter of fact, art and history have lost little by the fall of the Monasteries of San Jeronimo in Palma, or that of San Francisco in Barcelona which obstructed the neighbouring sea-wall; but why, in the name of history and in the name of art, could they not have preserved as historic monuments the Convent of Santa Catalina in Barcelona and the Dominican Monastery in Palma, whose aisles sheltered the tombs of the nobility, *'las sepulturas de personas de be',* as it is said in a small notebook which we had in our hands from the monastery archives? Listed in it were the tombs, and after the name of N. Cotoner, Grand-Master of Malta, occur those of Dameto, Muntaner, Villalonga, La Romana and *Bonapart!* This notebook, and everything that belonged to the Monastery, now belongs to the contractor who undertook to demolish it.

'This man, a typical Majorcan, whose manner is at first disturbing but soon sets you at ease by its charm, noticing the interest we took in these historic ruins and, like most of members of the lower classes, a great admirer of the great Napoleon, hastened to show us the tomb adorned with what Majorcan tradition claims to be the heraldic bearings of his Bonapart forefathers. We found this unusual enough to warrant a certain amount of research on the subject; but, being totally occupied with other work, we were unable to devote the time and the care needed for it completion.

'But we have traced the armorial bearings of the *Bonaparts*, which are:

'A quarter of azure, six gold stars arranged in pairs; and in the gules a gold spotted lion, a gold chief, an eagle nascent sable.

1º We took a facsimile of this coat of arms from a Spanish armigery, or book of heraldry, which was one of the very valuable objects found in the library of the Count of Montenegro.

2º In Barcelona, from a less exquisitely executed Spanish armigery belonging to the learned Archivist of Aragonese Crown, we find, dated the 15th June 1549, the proofs of the Fortuny family's noble extraction, in which appears, as one of their four quarterings, that of the maternal grandmother, who was a *Bonapart*.

'Mentioned in the register named *Index: Pedro III,* volume II of the archives of the Kingdom of Aragon, are two deeds dated 1276, relating to the *Bonpar* family. This name, which originated in either Provençal or Languedoc, would have become *Bonapart* when modified by the Majorcans, as were many others at that date.

'In 1411, *Hugo Bonapart,* a native of Majorca, went to the island of Corsica in the capacity of *Regent* or Governor for King Martin of Aragon; and the origin of the *Bonaparte,* or as they were later called, *Buonaparte,* is attributed to him; thus, *Bonapart* is the Romance name, *Bonaparte* the old Italian, and *Buonaparte* the modern Italian. It is known that members of Napoleon's family have signed themselves indifferently *Bonaparte* or *Buonaparte.*

'Who knows what importance these minor discoveries might have made a few years earlier, had they proved that Napoleon, who so much wanted to be French, had his origins in France.'

Not having the same political importance today, does not make M. Tastu's discovery less interesting, and if I had a voice in the allocation of Government funds designated to the Humanities, I should ensure this bibliographer the means of completing his research.

I agree that it matters very little now to establish Napoleon's French origins. This great commander, and to my mind (I apologize for this unfashionable judgement), not such a great prince, and because of his personality, most certainly a great man, well and truly adopted by France. Posterity will not ask whether his forebearers came from Florence, Corsica, Majorca or Languedoc; but historians will be interested in raising the veil that obscures this predestined family, where Napoleon's birth was no chance occurrence or isolated incidence. I am convinced that searching carefully among earlier generations of this family would reveal men and women well worthy of such offspring, and the coat of arms, these heraldic insignia which the Law of Equality has condemned, but which the historian must always regard as memorials of great significance, which may cast some light on the warlike and ambitious destiny of the earlier Bonapartes.

Yet was there ever a coat of arms more proud and more symbolic than that of those Majorcan knights? The lion in the attitude of combat, the star studded sky from which the prophetic eagle strives to break away, is it not the mysterious hieroglyph of an uncommon destiny? And Napoleon, who superstitiously loved the poetry of the stars, and who gave the eagle as an emblem to France, was he aware of his Majorcan escutcheon and being unable to trace his lineage to the original Bonpars of Provence, kept quiet about his Spanish ancestors? It is the fate of great men, after their deaths, to watch nations argue over their cradles or their tombs.

BONAPART

(Obtained from an armorial manuscript containing the coats of arms of the leading Majorcan families, etc. The manuscript belonged to Don Juan Dameto, the Majorcan chronicler who died in 1633, and is now kept in the library of the Count of Montenegro. It is a 16th century manuscript.)

Majorca, 20th September 1837

M. TASTU.

FORTUNY,

His father,
Majorcan lineage.

Field of silver, with
five black roundels,
two, two, and one.

COS,

His mother,
Majorcan lineage.

Field of gules (red),
a bear of gold, crowned
with a fleur-de-lys of
the same colour.

BONAPART,

His paternal grandmother,
Majorcan lineage.

The description of the
escutcheon is missing: the
dissimilarities result from
the fact that whoever
painted this, was not aware
of what he was copying; it
is also not accurate.

GARI,

His maternal grandmother,
Majorcan lineage.

Quartered in gules (red)
and azure (blue). Three
silver towers, two and one,
and three wavy bands
of silver.

Part Three

The Charterhouse of Valldemossa. (Pub. by Hetzel. Paris, 1856).

Chapter I

I T was a cloudless mid-December morning, caressed by the rays of an autumnal sun which soon was to become more and more uncommon, when we left for Valldemosa to take possession of our Carthusian cell. After crossing the fertile plains of Establiments, we reached an area wooded in parts, dry and stony in others, at times moist and cool, and changing its character everywhere with an abruptness that I have never seen anywhere else.

Nowhere else, except perhaps in some of the Pyrenean valleys, did Nature appear to me so free in all her charm as on these vast stretches of Majorcan heathland, and led me, with good reason, to doubt the Majorcan claim that the whole of their island has been fully cultivated.

However, I did not think of holding this against them, for nothing could be more beautiful than this neglected terrain which produces all that they desire, without need for more: twisted, bowed, wild trees; thorny brambles, splendid flowers; carpets of mosses and rushes, prickly caper-bushes, delicate and charming asphodels; all appearing in the forms God has given them, a ravine, a hill, a stony path ending abruptly in a quarry; a verdant track plunging into a deceptive stream, an open meadow coming to a sudden halt before the face of a craggy mountain; then brushwood strewn with great rocks seemingly fallen from the sky, sunken roads running alongside the torrent between bushes of myrtle and woodbine; and at last, a farmhouse, like an oasis in the heart of this wilderness, with its palm-tree, rising like a look-out, to guide the traveller on his lonely way.

Neither Switzerland nor the Tyrol had this appearance of free, primeval creation which charmed me so in Majorca. It seemed to me that in the wildest parts of the Swiss mountains Nature, having given in to the exceedingly rough atmospheric conditions, had escaped the hand of man only to meet with more rigorous intimidation from the heavens, and to rise like an impetuous spirit freed of itself, to become enslaved in it's own distress. In Majorca, she blooms beneath the kisses of a glowing sky, and smiles beneath the gusts of warm winds which glance over her as they wander the seas. Beaten down flowers spring up more sturdily than before; tree-trunks broken by the storm sprout more shoots than ever; and although there is, strictly speaking, no wilderness in Majorca, the lack of regular roads gives it an abandoned and mutinous look, resembling the beautiful Louisiana savannahs, where, in the cherished dreams of my youth, I used to follow René in search of the tracks of Atala or Chactas.

I am very sure that this eulogy will not please the Majorcans very much, for they claim their roads are very pleasant. Pleasant to look at, I won't deny; but as for being negotiable for vehicles, you shall judge yourselves.

The local hackney carriage is the *tartana,* a kind of postchaise drawn by a horse or a mule; or the *birlucho,* a kind of gig, which seats four and rests on its shafts like the tartana, both having solid wheels and massive iron fittings, and interiors upholstered with six inches of flock stuffing. Upholstery like that gives you something to think about when you climb for the first time into such a comfortable vehicle. The coachman sits on a small plank which acts as the driving seat, with his feet straddling the shafts while the animal runs between his legs, so that he always has the advantage of feeling each movement of the animal as well as every bump of the vehicle, as though he were riding his horse and driving his coach at the same time. However, he appears to be most content with this means of travelling, because he sings the whole time no matter how dreadfully jolted he is, and he only interrupts his song to utter some horrible curse when his animal hesitates before descending some steep precipice or balks at the thought of climbing a rocky wall.

This is how one journeys here: ravines, torrents, swamps, quickset hedges, ditches, all bar the path in vain; one does not stop for such trifles, because, of course they are part of the road.

On setting out, you take this obstacle course as a wager in bad taste, and you ask your guide what his game is.

'This is the road', he tells you.

'But this river?'

'It is part of the road.'

'And that deep hole?'

'It is part of the road.'

'And that bush?'

'It is all part of the road.'

'Fine!'

So you are left to your fate with no alternative but to resign yourself to your fate, bless the upholstery of the carriage without which your bones would surely be broken, commit your soul to God, and contemplate the scenery either in expectation of death or in hope of a miracle.

And yet you very often arrive safely and soundly, thanks to the steadiness of the carriage, the strength of the horse's legs, and perhaps also to the indifference of the coachman, who lets the animal find its own way while he sits with folded arms tranquilly smoking his cigar, while one wheel runs on a mountain and the other in a ravine.

One soon becomes accustomed to the danger on seeing others taking no notice of it: but the danger is very real. You do not overturn every day; but when you do you are seldom righted. A year before, on our road to Establiments, M. Tastu had experienced such an accident and had been left for dead where he lay. He later suffered from severe headaches which, however, did not dampen his desire to visit the island again.

Almost everyone on the island owns a carriage of some sort, and the nobility own those Louis XIV coaches, with bell mouthed boxes, some with as many as eight windows, and enormous wheels which defy all obstacles. These heavy, badly sprung, lumbering contraptions are spacious and strong and are nimbly drawn by four or six strong mules which carry you swiftly at a gallop and with incredible daring through the most terrible gorges, leaving you with a few bruises, some bumps on your head and aching joints.

The serious and humourless Miguel de Vargas, a typical Spanish author, writes in the following terms of the *horrorosos caminos* (horrible roads) of Majorca: 'One cannot sufficiently emphasize the neglect of this essential sector on this Balearic island. What they call a road is a chain of impassable precipices, and on the journey from Palma to the hills of Galatzo, the unfortunate traveller is confronted with death at every step.'

On the outskirts of towns and villages the roads are a little less perilous, but they have the serious disadvantage of being so narrowly confined between walls or ditches that two vehicles that meet cannot pass. When this happens, the oxen must be unhitched from the cart, or the horses from the carriage, and one of the vehicles must then be reversed, often for a long distance. Endless arguments arise as to who must reverse; during this delay one can do nothing better than repeat for his own edification the Majorcan motto: *Mucha calma.*

The Majorcans spend very little on the upkeep of their roads, but they have the advantage of possessing these in plenty. In fact, there is too great a choice. I travelled three times from the Charterhouse to Palma and back again; I took six different roads and on each occasion the driver of the *birlocho* lost his way and took us wandering up hill and down dale on the pretext of searching for the seventh road, said to be the best of all, which he never found.

It is three leagues from Palma to Valldemosa, but three Majorcan leagues which cannot be covered in under three hours of fast driving. The road rises imperceptibly for the first two; at the third, the road enters the mountains and leads to a well paved slope (possibly the former work of the Carthusian monks), which is very narrow, horribly steep and more dangerous than the rest of the way.

It is here that you begin to realize that you are on the Alpine side of Majorca; but however steeply the mountains rise on either side of the gorge and however fiercely the torrents race from boulder to boulder, it is only in the depth of winter that these regions take on that wild and untamed appearance ascribed to them by the Majorcans. In the month of December, despite the recent rains, the torrent was still no more than a delightful stream running through clusters of grass and flowers; the mountain smiled and the valley in which Valldemosa nestled opened before us like a spring garden.

To reach the Charterhouse, one has to walk; for no cart can climb the paved road which boldly wends its way through beautiful trees, while captivating scenery unfolds at each step, growing lovelier the higher one climbs. I have seen nothing more delightful, yet at the same time more melancholy, than these views where the varied tints of the holm-oak, carob-tree, pine, olive, poplar and cypress blend in dense bowers, profound depths of greenery, and the torrent plunges through sumptuously rich thickets of incomparable grace. I shall never forget a bend of the pass where, on glancing back, one saw, perched on a hill, one of those charming Arab cottages which I have already described, half hidden behind the prickly-pears and the silhouette of a tall palm-tree leaning over the chasm. When the mire and fog of Paris depress me, I close my eyes and see again, as in a dream, that verdant mountain, those tawny rocks and that solitary palm-tree lost in a rose-coloured sky.

The range of Valldemosa rises in a series of narrow plateaux to a sort of corrie formed by high mountains and closed on the

An old palm-tree, from the time of Chopin and George Sand.

northern side by the slope of the final plateau, at the entrance of which lies the monastery. The Carthusian monks, with vast labour, managed to soften the ruggedness of this romantic place. With terrace-walls, which left the view unobstructed, they converted the higher part of the valley into an enormous garden; a border of pyramidal cypresses, arranged in pairs on various levels, gives it the artificial look of a cemetery at the Opera.

This garden, planted with palms and almond-trees, occupies the whole slope of the valley, and rises in huge, ever-steepening terraces onto the lower slopes of the mountain. By moonlight, when their irregularity is hidden in shadow, it could be mistaken for an amphitheatre hewn out for contests between giants. In the middle, under a group of beautiful palm-trees, a stone reservoir collects the waters of the mountain springs and distributes them to the lower plateaux by means of conduits made of stone flags, similar to those that irrigate the countryside of Barcelona. This work is too extensive and ingenious, in Majorca as in Catalonia, to be the work of any nation except the Moors. They cover the whole interior of the island, and those which start from the Charterhouse garden, run beside the torrent bed and provide Palma with spring water throughout the year.

The Charterhouse, situated on the highest point, opens to the north overlooking a broad valley which widens as it slopes gently down on the other side of the hill towards the steep coastal cliffs, whose base is battered and eroded by the sea. One arm of the range goes off in the general direction of Spain; the other towards the east. Hence this picturesque Charterhouse commands views of the sea on both sides. From the north one hears the thunder of the waves, and one glimpses the faint shimmering line beyond the descending mountains and the vast plain unfolding to the south; it is a sublime picture, framed in the foreground by dark, fir covered rocks, the middle distance by bold mountains fringed with stately trees, the near background by rounded hillocks warmly gilded by the setting sun and on whose crests one can distinguish, though a league away, the outlines of microscopic trees, as fine as the antennae of a butterfly, but as black as the stroke of a pen in Indian ink on a field of sparkling gold. The luminous background is the plain; and at this distance, when the mountain mists begin to rise and cast a transparent veil over the depths, anyone could take it for the sea. But the sea lies still further away, and when the sun returns and the plain is like a blue lake, the Mediterranean confines this dazzling vista by tracing a strip of brilliant silver across it.

It is one of those views that completely overwhelm one, for it leaves nothing to be desired and nothing to the imagination. All that a poet or a painter might dream of, Nature has created here. Vast general effect, infinite detail, inexhaustible variety, blurred shapes, sharp outlines, hazy depths, they are all there and art can add nothing more. We are unable to always appreciate and understand the work of God, and if we reflect seriously upon ourselves, we realize the impossibility of ever expressing creatively this infinitude of life which enslaves and enthrals us. I should advise all those consumed by artistic vainglory to look well and often at such scenes. In this way I believe they will acquire a certain respect for the divine art that directs the eternal creation of things, a respect in which, as I judge from their vainglorious behaviour, they are singularly lacking.

As for myself, I never felt the emptiness of words more keenly than during my hours of meditation in the Charterhouse. I was often beset by fits of religious fervour, but the only words I could find to express my enthusiasm was: 'Oh God, blessed art Thou for having given me such good eyes!'

Yet I believe that while the occasional enjoyment of these sublime sights is refreshing and beneficial, permanent possession of them is dangerous. One grows accustomed to living under the influence of one's senses, and the abuse of sensuous indulgence is punished by the law of nervous irritation. This explains why monks, on the whole, take little note of the poetry of their monasteries, or peasants and shepherds in the beauty of their mountains.

Dans le bois d'oranges maurice et Solange s'emplissant d'oranges go jeun rendre malade.

valdemosa
mars 1839

A quaint drawing by Maurice, George Sand's son, in which he is seen with his sister, eating oranges in Valldemossa.

We ourselves had no time to lose interest, because almost every evening, at sunset, the mist would descend, hastening the close of day, which was already short enough in our little hollow. Until midday we were enveloped in the shadow of the high mountain to our left, and at three o'clock we fell into the shadow of the other high mountain to our right. But what beautiful plays of light we were able to study, when rays slanted through the crags or glided between the mountain ridges, and touched the middle-distance with crests of gold and purple! Sometimes our cypresses, black obelisks in the foreground, were bathed in this translucent glow; the clusters of dates on our palm-trees seemed like clusters of rubies, and a long line of shadow cut obliquely across the valley dividing it into two zones: one flooded with the light of summer, the other blue and cold as a winter landscape.

The Charterhouse of Valldemosa, which in accordance with the rules of the Carthusian Order, contained thirteen monks, including the Abbot, had escaped the destruction decreed in 1836 for all religious houses containing less than twelve inmates; but, like all the others, the community had been dissolved and the monastery itself suppressed and made over to the State. The Majorcan government, not knowing how to utilise these vast buildings, decided to let them crumble away, but in the meantime leased the cells to people as residences. In spite of the very reasonable rent, the villagers of Valldemosa had not chosen to take advantage of the offer, perhaps because of their profound piety and their regard for their monks, and perhaps also from superstitious fear: however, this did not stop them from going to dance there on carnival nights, as I shall later explain, and made them look askance on our irreverent presence within these venerable walls.

However, the greater part of the Charterhouse is inhabited, during the heat of summer, by the bourgeoisie of Palma who, at this altitude and beneath these thick vaults, find the air fresher than that of the plains or the city. But at the onset of winter, the

Valldemosan Peasants. Drawing by Maurice Sand.

pretty girl a few days before. The new husband was the only man condemned to dance the whole evening, approaching each of the women in turn, and dancing in front of her. No other man took the floor at all. During each duet the whole gathering, including the mayor himself, with his monk's cape and his great black, silver-headed staff, squatted solemnly and silently on the floor in the Oriental or African style.

The Majorcan *boleros* have an ancestral gravity and lack the worldly charm so admired in Andalusia. Men and women keep their arms extended and still, while their fingers drum the castanets without pause. The handsome Rafael danced until he had fulfilled his duty, and then squatted with the rest, whereupon the local devils had their hour of glory. One young lad, as thin as a wasp, aroused general admiration by the stiffness of his movements and his galvanic jumps, never moving from his place and never allowing a flicker of merriment to light up his face. A corpulent labourer, natty and very conceited, tried to kick out his legs with folded arms in the Spanish fashion, but he was sneered at, as he most certainly deserved, for his was the most ridiculous caricature imaginable. This country dance would have captivated us for a long time, had it not been for the smell of rancid oil and garlic which the ladies and gentlemen exuded, and which literally caught at one's throat.

We were less interested in the carnival disguises than in the traditional Majorcan costumes which are very elegant and most gracious. The women wear a white wimple made of lace or muslin, the *rebozillo*, which consists of two parts; one, which is fixed towards the back of the head, passing under the chin like a nun's coif, known as the *rebozillo en amunt*; and the other, the *rebozillo en volant*, flowing loosely like a cape over the shoulders. Their hair is smoothly parted in the middle, and caught behind in a long thick plait that emerges from the *rebozillo* to be tucked on one side into the belt. However, on normal working days, the hair is left unplaited and falls down the back in the *estufada*. The bodice is made of merino wool or black silk, low necked and with short sleeves, adorned above the elbows and on the back seams with jewelled buttons through which silver chains are stylishly threaded. They have slender waists, and tiny feet which are elegantly shod on feast days. Every simple village girl has lace stockings, satin shoes, a gold chain about her neck and several yards of silver chains drape about her waist and hanging from her belt. I saw many women with lovely bodies but few with lovely faces; they had the regular features which are to be found in Andalusia, but with a more frank and more gentle expression. In the Sollér district, which I did not visit, the women have a great reputation for their beauty.

The men whom I saw were not handsome, but at first sight all seemed so, because of their becoming costumes. On Sundays and holidays this consists of a multi-coloured silk waistcoat, heart-shape in cut and worn wide open, as is also the *sayo*, a short, close-fitting, buttonless black jacket, like a woman's bodice. An immaculate white shirt, caught at the neck and sleeves by bands of embroidery, leaves the throat bare and the chest covered with fine linen, which always sets off a costume to great advantage. The waist is tightly bound with a coloured sash, over wide, billowing, striped, Turkish-styled pantaloons made from locally produced cotton or silk. With this they wear white, black or fawn linen stockings and shoes of undressed, natural-coloured calf-skin. The wide-brimmed hat, made of wildcat's fur, or *moxine*, with cords and tassels of silk and gold thread, detracts from the Oriental flavour of this attire. At home they tie, turban-wise, a silk scarf or a printed calico handkerchief round their heads which suits them much better. During the winter they often wear a black woolen skull-cap over their tonsure; for they shave the crown of their head like priests, whether for a measure of cleanliness - and God knows it does not get them very far! - or whether for religious reasons. Their thick, coarse, frizzy hair flows (if a mane can be said to flow) about their necks. A fringe across their foreheads completes this medieval hair-style and gives a vigorous look to each face.

*Country dances in Valldemossa. The Charterhouse in the background.
Drawing by Maurice Sand.*

In the fields, their costume is less formal, but even more picturesque. Their legs are bare, or cased to the knees in tan leather gaiters, depending on the season. In hot weather they wear only a shirt and baggy pantaloons. In the winter they cover themselves in a grey cloak resembling a monk's habit, or in a huge African goat's skin, with the hair on the outside. When they go by in groups, wearing these long fawn-coloured skins, which fall from their heads to their feet with a black stripe running down the spine, they look from the rear like a herd of goats balancing on their hind legs. Nearly always, when they go out to the fields or come home again, one of them walks ahead playing the guitar or flute, and the others silently follow in step, with a look of cunning stupidity. By no means do they lack in shrewdness and only a complete fool would be deceived by their appearance.

They are generally tall, and their costumes tend to make them look slender, which makes them still even taller. Their necks, always uncovered, are fine and strong; their chests, free of tight waistcoats and braces, are open and well developed; but almost all have bandy-legs.

We noticed that the features of the older men, if not handsome, were at least serious and bore a certain air of nobility. They all resembled the monks we all so poetically imagined. The younger generation seemed to be of a more vulgar and lusty type, which seemed to show a break in the male line of descent. Is it really only twenty years that the monks ceased to interfere with the privacy of the home?

This is just a facetious observation of a traveller.

Majorcan Peasants. (J.B. Laurens). Pub. by J. Hetzel, 1856.

Chapter II

I had mentioned earlier that I was trying to discover the secret of monastic life in places where its traces were still fresh. Not that I expected to discover mysterious facts relating to this Charterhouse; I only asked that these abandoned walls would reveal the inner thoughts of those silent recluses, who for centuries had been separated from the life of their fellow-humans. I would have liked to have followed the frayed or broken thread of Christian faith in the souls thrown there by each generation, like a sacrifice to this jealous God whose need for human victims was as great as that of the pagan gods He had displaced. In short, I would have liked to revivify a Carthusian from the fifteenth century and one from the nineteenth, in order to compare the two Catholics - separated in their faith by an unfathomable abyss - by asking each what he thought of the other.

To reconstruct, with reasonable accuracy, the life of the medieval monk seemed easy enough. I saw him as a simple Christian, ardent, sincere, heart-broken at the spectacle provided by wars, the discord and the suffering of his contemporaries, fleeing from that abyss of evils to withdraw and separate himself as far as possible in ascetic meditation from a life where the perfectibility of the masses was a concept eluding the comprehension of the individual. But I found it more difficult to evoke the nineteenth century Carthusian, closing his eyes to the discernible and evident progress of humanity, indifferent to the lives of other men, understanding neither religion, the Pope, the Church, society nor himself, and seeing nothing more in the Charterhouse other than a spacious room, pleasant and safe, and in his vocation an assured existence with the opportunity to indulge his instincts with impunity, and a means of gaining, without merit, the respectful esteem of devout peasants and women. I was unable to estimate what degree of self reproach, blindness, hypocrisy, or insincerity he must have attained. It was impossible for him to have had real faith in the Roman Church, unless he was devoid of all intelligence. It was also impossible for him to have been a confirmed atheist, for then his life would have been an abominable lie, and I cannot believe that men can be so stupid or so evil. The idea of these inner conflicts, these choices between rebellion and submission, between philosophical doubt and superstitious dread, rose like a hell before my eyes; and the more I identified myself with this last Carthusian who had lived in my cell, the more strongly I felt the sufferings and anxieties I had ascribed to him weigh on my inflamed imagination.

It was enough to cast a glance at the old cloisters and compare them with the new to see how the increasing need for comfort, hygiene and even elegance had crept into the lives of these recluses; equally evident was the slackening of austerity, and the diminishment of mortification and penitence. Whereas all the old cells had been dark, cramped and draughty, the new ones were bright, airy and well built. A description of the cell we lived in will give an idea of how strict the Carthusian rule was, even when evaded and tempered as much as possible.

The cell was composed of three spacious, gracefully arched rooms, ventilated at the base by rosettes, each different and of a very graceful design. These three rooms were separated from the cloister by a dark entrance closed by a stout oak door. The wall was three feet thick. The middle room was intended for reading, prayer and contemplation and the only piece of furniture was a large combined praying-desk and grandfather-chair, about six to eight feet tall and firmly fixed to the wall. The room to the right was the Carthusian's bedroom; at the far end, in a low alcove, stood the bed with stone slabs piled above it in sepulchral style. To the left the workshop, dining room and store-room were to be found. A cupboard at the far end had a small wooden hatch which opened into the cloister through which this monk's food was passed in to him. His kitchen consisted of two small stoves placed outside, though no longer in the open air as the strict rule had prescribed. An arched porch, giving access to the garden, protected his culinary efforts from the elements, and allowed him to devote rather more time to this activity than the founder would have wished. A fireplace had been built into the third room, denoting further relaxations, but the architect had not been skilful enough to design a functioning chimney.

A long, narrow and dark passage, level with the rosettes and intended for ventilation, ran along the back of the cell, and a loft above it had been used for storing maize, onions, beans and other frugal winter provisions. On the south side, the three rooms opened on a small garden which occupied the same amount of space as they did, separated from its neighbours by ten foot walls and resting on a solidly built terrace overlooking an orange grove that spread from one end to the other end of the mountain tier immediately below. The tier below that was covered by a fine grape arbour, the third by almonds and palm-trees, and so on, down to the bottom of the valley which, as I have said before, resembled one huge garden.

To the right of each garden there was a cistern of dressed stone, three to four feet wide by as many deep, which received mountain waters from courses cut in the terrace balustrade. These waters were then distributed by means of stone channels which formed a cross dividing the garden into four equal squares. I could never understand why such an excessive amount of water should be needed to slake the thirst of one solitary man and irrigate a garden of twenty feet in diameter. Were it not that an abhorrence of bathing is a well-known characteristic of Catholic monks, and that Majorcan laymen are habitually abstemious in this respect, one might believe that these worthy Carthusians spent their whole lives bathing themselves like Indian priests.

This little garden, with its pomegranate, lemon and orange trees, surrounded by its raised brick paths, which were shaded like the cistern by fragrant arbours, looked like an elegant drawing room filled with flowers and greenery, where the monk could stroll on wet days and keep his feet dry, revive his lawns during the scorching heat with a sheet of running water, he could inhale, from the magnificent terrace, the fragrance of oranges, whose leafy tops put forth dazzling domes of flowers and fruit beneath his eyes, and could, in complete tranquillity, contemplate the landscape - a landscape, as I have said before, at once austere and full of grace, melancholy and magnificent. Finally he was able to grow rare and precious flowers to feast his eyes, pick the most succulent fruits to quench his thirst, listen to the sublime murmur of the sea, enjoy the splendour of a summer night beneath a perfect sky, and worship the Eternal God in the most beautiful temple which He has ever opened to man in the heart of Nature. Such seemed to me, at first, were the ineffable delights of the Carthusians; and such delights I promised myself as I settled into one of their cells, which seemed to have been designed to satisfy the magnificent and imaginative visions or dreams of a chosen host of poets and artists.

But when one envisages the life of a man lacking in intelligence and therefore unable to either dream or meditate, and perhaps without faith - that is to say, no fervour and no contemplation - buried in this cell, with solid walls that neither hear nor answer him, toughened by the hardships of the Rule and forced to observe its letter without understanding the spirit, condemned to the horror of isolation, reduced to catching distant glimpses, from the mountain heights, of mankind crawling along the valley-floor, remaining the eternal stranger to other captive souls, vowed to the self-same silence, locked in the same tomb, always neighbours but always apart, even in prayer; finally when one feels one's own self, a free and rational being, sympathetically guided into certain terrors and certain failings, everything becomes gloomy and sombre, shrouding a life of emptiness, error and impotence.

Then one understands the immeasurable boredom of this monk on whom Nature has lavished her loveliest display, who does not delight in it, for he has no one with whom to share his enjoyment; the brutish melancholy of the penitent who, like a plant, no longer suffers anything except extremes of cold and heat; and the mortal chill of the Christian in whom nothing can reanimate or revive the spirit of asceticism. Condemned to eat alone, work alone, suffer and pray alone, he must surely have had one desire left, to escape from this appalling confinement; and I was told that the last Carthusians felt so little for it that they absented themselves for weeks and months on end, and the Prior was powerless to recall them to the Order.

I am afraid that in my lengthy and detailed description of our Charterhouse, I have not conveyed the least notion of the enchantment it at first held for us, an allure which lost its appeal on closer examination. As usual, I have allowed my memories to take over, and now after having conveyed my impressions, I ask myself why I could not have said in twenty lines what I have said in twenty pages, and to know that peace of mind and freedom from care and all that that includes, at first seems delightful to the weary spirit, but with reflection the charm disappears. Only a genius can create a complete and lively picture with a single stroke of the brush. When M. Lamennais visited the *Camaldules* at Tivoli, he was overcome by the same feeling, and expressed it in a masterly fashion:

"We arrived there," he wrote, "at the hour of communal prayer. To us they all seemed well advanced in age, and taller than the average. After the office they remained kneeling in two rows along one side of the nave, motionless and in deep meditation.

They no longer seemed to form part of this earth; their shaven heads bowed beneath thoughts and preoccupations other than ours; wrapped in their long white cloaks like the praying statues of old tombs, they made no movement and showed no outward sign of life.

"We can well understand the attraction this solitary life has for certain world-weary, disillusioned souls. Who has not aspired to something similar? Who has not turned his eyes more than once towards the desert and dreamed of peace in a remote corner of a forest, or mountain grotto near an unknown spring where the birds of the air come to slake their thirst?

"But this is not the true destiny of man: man is born for action; he has a task to fulfil. What matter, if it be hard? Is he not faced with the duty of Love?"

(Affaires de Rome.)

Having been so impressed with this brief passage, filled with images, aspirations, profound ideas and thoughts, accidentally thrown between M. Lamennais's account of his experiences at the Holy See, I am sure that one day some great painter will make it the subject of a painting. On one side, the *Camaldules* at prayers, mysterious, peaceful monks, for ever useless, for ever powerless, bowed spectres, the last manifestations of a cult about to be lost in the darkness of the past, as cold and gloomy as the tombstones they are kneeling on; on the other, the man of the future, the last priest, revitalized by the Church's final spark of genius, brooding on the fate of these monks, observing them with an artist's eye, judging them philosophically. Here, the Levites of Death motionless under their shrouds; there, the Apostle of Life, an indefatigable traveller through the endless fields of thought, already bidding a sympathetic farewell to the poetry of the cloister, shaking the dust of the Papal city from his feet, to stride forth along the blessed road of moral freedom.

I have not been able to gather any historical facts about our Charterhouse, save for a sermon preached by St. Vincent Ferrier in Valldemossa, and once again I am indebted to M. Tastu for the correct account. This sermon became the most important event of the year 1413, and it is interesting to learn with what eagerness a missionary could be welcomed at that time, and with what solemnity he was received.

"In the year 1409, the Majorcans, gathered in a great assembly, decided to write to Master Vincent Ferrer, or Ferrier, inviting him to come and preach in Majorca. It was Don Luis de Prades, Bishop of Majorca, *camerlingo* of Pope Benedict XIII, (the Anti-pope Peter de Luna) who, in 1412 wrote a letter to the aldermen of Valencia begging the apostolic aid of Master Vincent and who, in the following year, embarked with him in Barcelona and set sail for Palma. The day after his arrival, the saintly missionary started preaching and organized nocturnal processions. A great drought reigned over the island, but after Master Vincent's third sermon the rains began to fall. This is how the Royal Procurator, Don Pedro de Casaldaguila reported this information to King Ferdinand:

'Most High, Most Excellent Prince and Victorious Lord:
'I have the honour of informing you that Master Vincent arrived in this city on the first day of September, being welcomed with due solemnity. On Saturday morning he preached to an enormous crowd, who heard him with such devotion that now every night there are processions in which men, women and children can be seen scourging themselves. And since no rain had fallen for a long time, the Lord God, moved by the prayers of the children and the people, wished that this Realm, which was dying of the drought, should see fall, after the third sermon, an abundant rain throughout the island, where at the inhabitants rejoiced greatly.

'May Our Lord God grant you many years of life, Most Victorious Lord, and exalt your Royal Crown!

Majorca, September 11th, 1413'

"The crowds that wished to hear the missionary increased to such an extent, that they could not be accommodated in the huge church of the convent of St. Dominic, so the large gardens of the convent were handed over to them where stands were set up and walls knocked down.

"St. Vincent Ferrier preached in Palma until October 3rd, when he left to visit the island. His first stop was in Valldemossa, where he was received and lodged in the monastery, and which he doubtless chose out of respect for his brother Boniface, then General of the Carthusian Order. The prior of Valldemossa had come to Palma to fetch him. The church of Valldemossa was less capable to contain the crowds than that of Palma.

"Here is the chronicler's record:

'The town of Valldemossa remembers the time when St. Vincent Ferrier sowed the word of God. Within the bounds of the said town lies the estate called *Son Gual*; the missionary made his way there, followed by a countless multitude. There was a wide and level field, and the hollow trunk of a huge and ancient olive tree served him as a pulpit. While the saint was preaching from the old olive tree, it started to rain heavily. The Devil, author of winds, lightning and thunder, seemed to wish the congregation to disperse and take cover, which some had already started doing when St. Vincent ordered them not to move and began to pray. Immediately a cloud spread like a canopy over him and those who were listening; while those who had continued to work in a neighbouring field were compelled to abandon their work.

'The ancient tree-trunk was still in existence less than a century ago; for our fore-fathers had preserved it with great care. Later, the heirs of the *Son Gual* estate neglected to care for this sacred relic and its history was forgotten. But God did not wish that St. Vincent's crude pulpit should be lost. Some servants of the estate, going out to chop wood, caught sight of the old olive and wanted to hew it in pieces, but their axes immediately broke; and when the news reached the ears of the older inhabitants, the cry of a miracle went up, and the sacred olive was spared. Later it came to pass that this tree split into thirty-four pieces; and although they were near the town, no one dared touch them for they were respected as relics.'

"The holy preacher carried the word of God to the smallest villages, healing the sick in body and spirit. The water of a spring which rises near Valldemossa was the only remedy prescribed by the saint. This spring is still known under the name of *Sa Bassa Ferrara.*

"St. Vincent spent six months on the island before he was recalled by King Ferdinand of Aragon to help him repair the schism which was afflicting the West. The saint took leave of the Majorcans on February 22nd, 1414, in Palma Cathedral; and after blessing the congregation, he set off to the port, accompanied by jurors, noblemen and a great multitude of common people, performing many miracles on the way; as the chroniclers record and as tradition still perpetuates it in the Balearic Islands."

This account, which would bring a smile to the lips of Miss Fanny Elssler,[20] gives rise to an observation made by M. Tastu, which is interesting in two respects: firstly, he provides a very reasonable explanation for one of the miracles of St. Vincent Ferrier, and secondly, because he confirms an important fact in linguistic history. Here is his note:

"Vincent Ferrier wrote his sermons in Latin, but he pronounced them in the Limousine tongue. This power he possessed of enabling his congregations to understand him although he spoke to them in a foreign language, was looked on as miraculous. However, there was nothing more natural if one bears in mind the age when Master Vincent flourished. At that time, the

---

[20] 1810-1884. The famous Viennese ballet dancer, contemporary to the authoress and a fierce rival to the dancer Taglioni. *(Translator's note.)*

Romance languages of the three great regions, the North, the Centre, and the South, were, with some small differences, almost identical; the people, and especially the educated classes, understood one another very well. Master Vincent had great success in England, Scotland, Ireland, Paris, Brittany, Italy, Spain and the Balearic Islands; for in all these countries the inhabitants understood, even if they could not speak it, a Romance language, which was the sister, parent or cousin of the Valencian language, Vincent Ferrier's mother tongue.

"Besides, was not the famous missionary a contemporary of Chaucer, Jean Froissart, Christine de Pisan, Boccaccio, Ausias March, and many other European celebrities?" [21]

---

[21] The people of the Balearic Islands speak Limousine, an ancient romance language; a language which M. Raynouard has included, without research or discrimination, into the Provençal. Of all the Romance languages, Majorcan has suffered fewer changes than any other, being centred in its islands where it is kept clean from all foreign contamination. The Langue d'Oc, even in its present decadent condition as the pleasing dialect of Montpellier and its environments, offers the closest analogy to the old and modern Majorcan. This is explained by the frequent sojourns of the kings of Aragon and their courts to the city of Montpellier. Pedro II, killed at Muret in 1213 while fighting Simon de Monfort, had married Marie, daughter of a Count of Montpellier, and had had a son James I, surnamed the Conqueror, who was born in Montpellier and who had spent his early years there. One of the characteristics which distinguishes Majorcan from other Romance dialects of the South of France, are the definite articles in popular use, most of these occur also in certain districts of the Island of Sardinia. Besides the neuter definite article *lo*, the masculine *el*, and the feminine *la*, we find the following:

Masc. sing.	so	sa	sos	sas
Fem. sing.	so	sa	sos	sas
Masc. plural	es	es	ets	ets
Fem. plural	en	na	ens	nas

However, in passing we should remark that these articles, although of ancient use, have never been employed in the legal documents dating from the Arogonese conquest of the Balearics; that is to say that on these islands, as in the Italic lands, two languages reigned simultaneously: the uneducated tongue, *plebea*, used by the people (this sees little change); and the language of scholarship and literature, *aulica illustra*, which the passage of time, the progress of civilization, or the works of a genius, has purified and improved. Thus, today, Castillian is the literary language of Spain; yet each province keeps its specific dialect for everyday use. In Majorca, Castillian is used only on formal occasions; normally you will hear only Majorcan, whether spoken by the people or by the nobility. If you pass under a balcony where a young girl, an *Atlote* (from the Arabic *aila, lella*) is watering her flowers, it is in her soft native language that you will hear her singing:

> *Sas atlotes, tots es diumenges,*
> *Quant no tenen res mes que fer,*
> *Van a regá es claveller,*
> *Dient-li: 'Beu jà que no menjes!'*

The young girls every Sunday
When they have nothing better to do,
Go watering the carnation pot,
And tell it: 'Drink, since you do not eat!'

The music which accompanies the words of the young girl has a Moorish rhythm, in a key whose mournful cadences touch your heart and set you dreaming. But the girl's mother has heard her and is swift to reply:

> *'Atlotes, filau! filau!*
> *Que sa camya se riu;*
> *Y sino l'apadassau,*
> *No v's arribar' à estiu!'*

Girls, spin, spin!
For your shift is splitting (literally: 'the shift is smiling')
And you will have to patch it
If you want it to last the summer!'

Majorcan, especially when spoken by women has, for the foreigners ear, a gentle and graceful charm all of its own. When a woman says good-bye, using the following words: *'Bona nit tenga! Es meu cô no basta per dir li: Adios!'* 'Good night! I do not have the heart to say: Good-bye!' it seems as if the soft cantilena could be recorded as a musical phrase.

After these examples of the Majorcan vernacular, I would like to quote an example of the old academic language. The *Mercader mallorqui* (The Majorcan Merchant), a fourteenth century troubadour who sings of the cruelties of his lady and takes leave of her thus:

> *Çercats d'uy may, jà siats bella e pros,*
> *'quels vostres pres, e laus, e ris plesents,*
> *Car vengut es lo temps que m'aurets mens.*
> *No m'aucirá vostre 'sguard amoros,*
> > *Ne le semblança gaya;*
> > *Car trobat n'ay*
> > *Altra qui m'play*
> > *Sol que lui playa!*
> *Altra, sens vos, per que l'in volray bé,*
> *E tindr' en car s'amor, que 'xi s' convé.*

Although lovely and noble, you may henceforth search
For such merits, such praises, such charming smiles which were yours alone,
For the time is come when you shall seldom have me at your side,
Your amorous look shall no longer slay me,
Nor your pretended gaiety;
For I have found
Another who pleases me,
But might I please her!
Another, for unlike you, will be pleased with me
For whom love is dear, so that is what I shall do

The Majorcans, like all Southern people are natural poets and musicians, or as their ancestors called them, 'troubadours', *trobadors*, which could be translated by 'improvisers'. The Island of Majorca still has some, who enjoy a well-deserved reputation, two of whom live in Sóller. These troubadours are frequently visited by happy or unhappy lovers. For a fee and with the relevant information, they stand beneath the girls' balconies, at a late hour of the night, and sing improvised *coplas* of praise, complaint, and sometimes even abuse. Foreigners may also avail themselves to this pleasure, it is not regarded as a matter of any consequence on this island. *(Notes by M. Tastu).*

Chapter III

I cannot continue my narrative without quoting an extract from the ecclesiastical records of Valldemossa; for, before discussing the fanatical piety of the villagers with whom we had had contact, I must describe the saint who is their great pride and whose simple cottage they showed us.

"Valldemossa is also home to Catalina Tomás, who was beatified in 1792 by Pope Pius VI. Several biographies have been written of this holy virgin, the most recent being that of Cardinal Antonio Despuig. The story has some delightfully naive features. God, so the legend runs, had blessed His handmaiden with reasoning far beyond her years, and she was seen to rigorously observe days of fasting long before reaching the age at which the Church ordains such observance. From her earliest infancy she abstained from having more than one meal a day. Her devotion to the Passion of the Redeemer, and the Sorrows of His Blessed Mother were so fervent that on country walks she always recited her rosary, using the leaves of the olive-trees and the lentisk to count the tens. Her love for seclusion and her enjoyment of religious exercises, coupled with a dislike of dances and other worldly amusements, soon won her the name of *'viejecita'*, or 'little old woman'.[22] But her solitude and abstinen-

---

[22] George Sand is mistaken. Catalina Tomás was called *'Beateta'* - 'The Little Saint', and not *'Veyata'* the Majorcan for *'viejecita'* - 'little old woman'. *(Translator's note.)*

ce were rewarded by visits from the angels and the celestial court: Jesus Christ, His Mother and the Saints came to serve her, Mary nursed her in illness; St. Bruno lifted her when she fell; St. Anthony guided her through the darkness of night, carrying her pitcher and filling it at the fountain; St. Catherine, her patron saint, dressed her hair and cared for her like a vigilant and devoted mother; St. Cosmo and St. Damian healed the wounds that she received in her struggles with the Devil, for her victory was not won without a fight; and finally, St. Peter and St. Paul were always at her side to help and defend her in temptation.

"She entered the convent of St. Magdalen in Palma, where she embraced the Order of St. Augustine, becoming an exemplary penitent, and, as the Church chants in its prayers, obedient, poor, chaste and humble. Her biographers attribute to her the power of prophecy and the gift of miracles. It is said that one day, at a time when public prayers were being offered in Majorca for the health of Pope Pius V, Catalina interrupted them suddenly, to announce that they were no longer needed, for at that very hour, the Pontiff had departed from this world, which proved to be true.

"She died on the 5th of April 1574, uttering the Psalmist's words: 'Lord, into Thy hands I commend my spirit!'

"Her death was regarded a public disaster, and she was paid the highest honours. A devout Majorcan lady, Doña Juana de Pochs, replaced the wooden coffin, in which the holy virgin had originally been laid, by a splendid alabaster sepulchre ordered from Genoa; in addition she also made a bequest for masses to be said both on the anniversary of the Blessed Catalina's death and on the day of her patron, St. Catherine; and also instructed that a lamp be kept perpetually burning on her tomb.

"The body of this blessed virgin is preserved today[23] in the

---

[23] The body of Catalina Tomás, now a saint, lies in the convent of Santa Magdalena in Palma. Her body is still occasionally displayed to the faithful. The fact that her body did not decompose, was taken as one more proof of her holiness. *(Translator's note.)*

convent of the parish of Santa Eulalia where Cardinal Despuig consecrated an altar and a religious service to her."[24]

I have gladly related this little legend, for it does not enter my mind to deny the existence of such a thing as holiness, namely the true holiness possessed by fervent souls. Although the ardour and visions of a little girl from the Valldemossan mountains no longer have the same religious meaning and philosophical value as the inspirations and ecstasies of the Saints of the Golden Age of Christianity, the *Viejecita Tomása* is none the less closely related to the romantic shepherdess, St. Genevieve and the sublime shepherdess, St. Joan of Arc. At no time has the Roman Church refused to honour in the Heavenly Kingdom the humblest children of the people, but times have come where she has condemned and rejected those of her apostles who try to improve their existence in this earthly kingdom. The *pagesa*[25] Catalina was *obedient, poor, chaste and humble*: but the Valldemossan *pagès* have profited so little from her example, and understood so little of her life, that one day they tried to stone my children for they regarded as desecration the fact that my son was sketching the ruins of the Charterhouse. They behaved exactly like the Church, with one hand they kindled the auto-da-fé pyres, and with the other they burned incense before the effigies of her saints.

The village of Valldemossa[26] has proudly claimed the status of a town since Moorish days. It lies in the lap of the mountain, level with the Charterhouse of which it appears to be an annexe. The houses perch, like a cluster of sea-swallow nests, in an almost inaccessible spot, and the inhabitants, for the most part fishermen, leave their homes at dawn and do not return until

---

[24] Notes of M. Tastu.

[25] *Pagés, pagesa,* is the name of the second caste of men and women in Majorca; the first, *ès cavallers,* was that of the cavaliers and nobles; the second, *ès pagesos,* the farmers; the third, *ès menastrals,* the artisans. All who inhabited the country and worked the lands were called *pagés.*

[26] The Moors called it Villa-Avente, a Roman name which, I believe, had been given it by the Pisans or the Genoese. *(M. Tastu)*

night. All day long the village is filled with the most talkative women in the world, who sit on their doorsteps busily mending their husband's breeches, a task that resembles his net-mending, and singing at the top of their voices. They are as religious as the men, but their devotion is less intolerant and more sincere. In this, here as everywhere else, the female sex is superior. Generally speaking, women devote themselves to religious observances from enthusiasm, habit or conviction, whereas with men it is more often a matter either of ambition or advantage. France offered clear enough proof of this under the reigns of Louis XVIII and Charles X, when all major and minor positions in the government or in the army could be bought at the price of a confessional note or a mass.

The Majorcans' attachment to the monks is based on greed; in order to understand this, I shall quote M. Marliani, whose opinions are reliable, because this historian of modern Spain shows himself hostile to the sudden expulsion of the monks in 1836.

"Being mindful landowners," he writes, "and not paying great attention to their wealth, the monks had built up a genuine understanding between the peasants and themselves; tenant-farmers working the monastery lands suffered little hardship regarding the amount of rent, or its regular collection. The monks, having no posterity to consider, did not amass their revenue, and once their estates produced enough to meet the material needs of their community, they were most generous with the remainder. Therefore, the sudden and forcible expropriation of the monks' properties really upset the peasants' economy; they understood only too well that the Government and their new landlords would demand more of them than had a brotherhood of parasites without family or social ties. The beggars who swarmed about the refectory doors were no longer given the leftovers from the monastery tables."

Carlism among the Majorcan peasants can be accounted for on material grounds only; for no province was less bound to

Spain by feelings of patriotism, nor a people less inclined to political participation. At the core of all the secret prayers they offered for the restoration of the ancient regime, was the fear of any new upheaval, what ever it might be; the alarm which, at the time of our stay, had caused the island to be placed in a state of siege, frightened both the upholders of Don Carlos and the supporters of Queen Isabella. This alarm was characteristic, not so much of the Majorcans cowardice (for I am sure they would make very good soldiers), but more of anxiety regarding their property and their egoistic desire to see their peace undisturbed.

An old priest dreamed one night that robbers were breaking into his house. Terrified by the nightmare, he awoke, leapt out of bed and roused his housekeeper. She, sensing his terror, although ignorant of what had caused it, wakened the whole neighbourhood with her screams. Fear spread quickly through the village, and thence throughout the island. News was rife that a Carlist army had landed. The Captain-General heard the evidence of the priest who, whether ashamed to retract what he had said, or still suffering, maintained that he had seen the Carlists. Measures were at once taken to meet the danger: a state of siege was declared in Palma, and the military forces of the island were put on stand-by.

But nothing materialized, no bush stirred and no foreign footprint, as on Robinson Crusoe's island, was left on the sandy shores. The wretched priest was severely punished by the authorities for having made them look foolish, and, instead letting him off for being a dreamer, they imprisoned him as an instigator to agitation. Yet the precautionary measures were not lifted and, when we left Majorca, at the time of the Maroto executions, the state of siege still remained in force.

How strangely secretive the Majorcans seemed in face of such events that convulsed Spain. Nothing was said, unless in a whisper in his own family circle. It was extraordinary that in a country so free of wickedness and oppression, such mistrust reigned. I have never read anything quite as absurd as the Palma newspaper articles, and I still regret that I did not bring away a few copies as examples of Majorcan polemics. But here, without exaggeration, is the sort of comment made on the significance and authenticity of the latest news items:

'However true these events may appear in the eyes of those ready to believe them, we cannot too strongly recommend that our readers await the sequel before passing any judgement. The thoughts which spring to mind in the face of such events call for mature consideration on our part, and at the same time a certainty which, though we do not wish to cast doubt on it, we will neither imprudently anticipate. The fate of Spain is cloaked in a veil which will soon be lifted, but on which no one must lay an ill-advised hand before the decisive hour. Until then we shall refrain from giving our opinion, and shall advise all discerning minds to withhold their opinions on the actions of the various parties, until they see the situation acquire clearer outlines.' etc.

Caution and reserve, as the Majorcans themselves admit, are the predominant traits of their character. In the countryside a peasant will always acknowledge a greeting; but should someone he does not know address him with an additional word, even in his own dialect, he will be most reluctant to reply. A foreign air is enough to scare him, and he will do all he can to avoid an encounter.

We could have lived on good terms with these worthy people, had we only put on an appearance at Church. This would not have prevented them from holding us to ransom on every conceivable excuse, but we should have at least been able to walk through their fields without the risk of being hit on the head by a stone as we passed some bushes. Unfortunately, it did not immediately occur to us to take this precautionary measure, and we remained unaware of how profoundly our way of life had shocked them until almost the end of our stay. They called us heathens, Mohammedans - or Jews, which they believed to be the worst of all. The Mayor warned them against us; and I would not have been surprised if the priest had preached against us. They were so deeply scandalized by my daughter's blouse and trousers. They found it disgraceful that a *young person*, nine years of age, should roam the mountains *disguised as a man*. And it was not only the peasants who were affected by this prudishness.

The cowherd's horn, which on Sundays resounded through the village and along the roads, calling the dawdlers to mass, met with no response from us in the Charterhouse. At first we were deaf through a failure to understand, but once we understood, we became even deafer. They then proceeded to avenge the glory of God in a most un-Christian manner. They banded together and refused to sell us their fish, eggs or vegetables except at an exorbitant price. We were unable to quote market prices or normal values. At the slightest objection, the peasant, with the air of a Spanish grandee, would reply: "You don't want any? Then you won't have any!" and returning the onions or potatoes into his sack, he would retire in a most dignified fashion and could not be recalled to reach an agreement. Our punishment for bargaining was to go hungry.

It was most effective, for we went hungry. These peasants would not undersell one another. The next man asked twice as much as the first, and the third three times as much, so we found ourselves at their mercy and were forced to live like hermits, paying more than would have kept us in princely style in Paris. Our saviour was the consul's chef in Palma, who kept us supplied with food, and had I been a Roman Emperor, I should have set his cotton cap among the constellations. But on wet days no carrier would risk venturing out, at any price; and since it rained for two months, we often had bread as hard as a ship's biscuit and dined like true Carthusians.

This would have been of minor consequence had we all been in good health. I eat sparingly and am almost stoical in my diet. My children's magnificent appetites let them eat anything and everything. My son, who had been sick and weakly when we arrived, had made a miraculous recovery and cured a dangerous rheumatic complaint by romping from dawn to dusk, like a freed hare through the tall mountain plants, soaked to the waist. Providence, with the grace of Nature, had worked these wonders for him.

However, our other invalid, far from improving on the hardships and the damp, had fallen into an alarming decline. Although he had been condemned as a hopeless case by the whole medical faculty of Palma, he had no chronic complaint whatsoever; but the after-effects of a cold and the absence of a nutritious diet, had plunged him into a listless condition from which he could not emerge. He resigned himself to this, as one can do if the suffering is one's own; but we could not resign ourselves to see him suffer, and for the first time in my life I became seriously irritated by trifling annoyances. I would loose my temper when the soup was too peppery or had been dipped into by the servant, or because the fresh bread had not arrived or had been turned into a sponge while the mule forded the torrent. I certainly do not remember what I ate in Pisa or Trieste, but if I live to be a hundred, I shall never forget the arrival of the basket of provisions at the Charterhouse. What would I have given to have a daily cup of soup and a glass of Bordeaux to offer to our invalid! Majorcan food and the manner in which it was prepared when we did not supervise and assist in the cooking, filled him with loathing. Up to what point was this justified? One day, when a skinny chicken was served at the table, we saw a number of huge *Herrenflöhe* hopping on its steaming back. Hoffman might have presented them as malign spirits, but he certainly would not have eaten them in the sauce. My children, overcome by laughter at this sight, nearly fell under the table.

The basis of all Majorcan cooking is invariably the pig, in every conceivable form and manner of presentation. It might be well to quote the Little Chimney-sweep, who, when praising his inn, said admiringly that five kinds of meat were eaten there:

pig, pork, lard, ham and bacon. I am sure that over two thousand different pork dishes are prepared in Majorca, and at least two hundred kinds of black pudding and all so seasoned with garlic, black and red pepper and other corrosive spices, that you risk your life with each mouthful. Twenty dishes appear on the table, looking like any Christian food: but take heed, for they are hellish concoctions brewed by the Devil himself. Finally, for dessert, a fine pastry tart arrives with slices of fruit resembling sugared oranges. This turns out to be a garlic-flavoured pork-tart with slices of *tomatiges* (tomatoes) and sweet peppers, all sprinkled with white salt which you have mistaken for powdered sugar. There are numerous chickens, but they are all skin and bone. In Valldemossa we should doubtless have been taxed a *réal* for every grain of corn we bought to fatten them. The fish they brought from the sea was as tasteless and dry as were the chickens.

One day, for the sake of examining it, we bought a large *calamar* (squid). I have never seen a more horrible creature. Its body was the size of a turkey with eyes as big as oranges, and its floppy, repulsive tentacles, when uncurled, were four or five feet long. The fishermen assured us that it was a great delicacy. We were not tempted by its appearance, but paid homage to Maria Antonia for the way she prepared and ate it with such gusto.

If our excitement over the squid caused these worthy folk to smile, we had our chance a few days later. Coming down the mountain we saw the *pagesos* leaving their tasks and rushing towards a group of people who had halted in the road and were carrying a basket containing a pair of wonderful, extraordinary, marvellous, incomprehensible birds. The entire population of the mountain was in a state of excitement at the appearance of this unknown species of fowl.

'What do they eat?' they asked, gazing at them.

'Perhaps they don't eat at all!' someone answered.

'Do they live on land or sea?'

'They probably spend all the time in the air.'

The two birds had nearly been suffocated by the general admiration before we discovered that they were neither condors, phoenixes, nor hippogryphs, but two fine geese which a wealthy squire was sending as a gift to a friend.

In Majorca, as in Venice, liqueur wines are plentiful and exquisite. Normally we drank a muscatel wine which was as good and as inexpensive as the Cyprian wine of the Adriatic coast. But the red wines, the correct preparation of which is an art unknown in Majorca, were harsh, very dark, burning, of a high alcoholic content and far more expensive than the simplest table wines of France. These hot, heady wines were not good for our invalid, neither for us, so we nearly always drank the water, which was excellent. I do not know if it was the purity of the spring water that produced a noticeable change in us: our teeth acquired a whiteness that no cosmetician could have given to the most fastidious Parisian. Perhaps the cause lay in our forced abstemiousness.

Having no butter and being unable to stomach the fats, the nauseating oils and the charred methods of native cooking, we lived on lean meat, fish and vegetables. Instead of sauce, we seasoned with water from the torrent which, as an occasional treat, was flavoured with the juice of a sour orange freshly picked from our garden. On the other hand, our desserts were splendid: candied sweet potatoes from Malaga, candied pumpkin from Valencia, and grapes worthy of the land of Canaan. These grapes, white and pink, are oblong and covered with a thick skin which helps preserve them throughout the winter. They are exquisite, and you can eat as many of them as you like without suffering from the flatulence that ours produce. The grapes from Fontainebleau are juicier and fresher; those of Majorca are sweeter and fleshier. The latter are to be eaten, the former are to be drunk. A painter would have admired these grapes, for some bunches weighed between twenty and twenty-five pounds. They were our sustenance in times of food shortage. The peasants believed that they had sold them to us well, charging four times their value; but little did they know that this was still nothing compared to the price of our grapes, so we both had the pleasure of laughing at one another. With regard to the prickly-pears, there was never an argument; it is by far the most horrible fruit I ever tasted.

If these frugal conditions had not, as I have mentioned before, produced a harmful, even fatal, effect on one of us, the others would have found them bearable enough. We had managed, even in Majorca, even in a deserted Charterhouse, even while at loggerheads with the most cunning of peasants, to surround ourselves with some degree of comfort. We had window-panes, doors, and a stove, a unique stove which the best blacksmith in Palma had taken a month to forge, and which cost us a hundred francs. It was a simple iron cylinder with a pipe that led out of the window. It took a good hour to light, and then it quickly turned red-hot; so, after having kept the windows open all the time to clear the room of smoke, they had to be opened again to let the heat escape. Besides, the so-called stove-maker had lined the interior, by way of cement, with a by-product of the cow with which, for religious reasons, Indians plaster their homes and sometimes their bodies; the cow is, as we well know, regarded by them as a sacred animal. However purifying this saintly odour may be for the soul, I can testify that it is, while burning, far from a delight to the senses. For the month it took for the cement to dry out, it was easy for us to imagine that we were in that circle of the Inferno where Dante claimed to have seen the sycophants. In vain I searched my memory for the sin I had committed to warrant such torment, what Power I had flattered, which Pope or King I had encouraged in his errors. In my conscience I could find neither office-boy nor porter, not even a bow to a policeman or a journalist!

Luckily, the Carthusian apothecary could sell us some exquisite gum-benzoin, left over from the stock of perfumes which, not so long ago, was burned as incense before the Divine image in his monastery church; and this heavenly emanation conquered the fumes of the Inferno's eighth trench.

We had magnificent furniture: impeccable trestle-beds; clean, new mattresses, not very soft and more expensive than in Paris; those fine large coverlets of quilted and padded chintz, bought at a reasonable price from the Jews in Palma. A French lady, living on the island, was good enough to let us have several pounds of feathers, which she had ordered for her own use from Marseilles, and with which we made two pillows for our invalid. This was indeed a great luxury in a country where geese are looked upon as fantastic creatures, and chickens still itch when they are lowered from the spit.

We had several tables, many straw bottomed chairs similar to those seen in our country cottages; a voluptuous deal sofa with cushions of wool-stuffed ticking. The uneven and crumbling floor of the cell was covered with those long-strawed Valencian mats which resembled a lawn yellowed by the sun, and those splendid long-haired sheepskins, of fine quality and whiteness, which they know very well how to dress here.

As in Africa and the Orient, there are few cupboards in the old houses of Majorca, and none at all in the Carthusian cells. Their possessions were stored in great deal chests. Our yellow leather trunks could pass for elegant pieces of furniture. A large, multi-coloured tartan shawl, used as a foot-rug on our journey, now became a sumptuous curtain screening the alcove, and my son decorated the stove with one of those charming clay vases, in pure Moorish style, from Felanitx.

Felanitx is a Majorcan village which should supply Europe with its beautiful jars, which are so light that one would think they were made of cork, and of so fine a texture as to seem like some precious metal. These small exquisitely formed pitchers are used as carafes, and keep water wonderfully cool. The clay is so porous that in less than half a day the water seeps out, leaving the jar empty. I am no physicist, and perhaps my remarks may seem naive; but I thought it marvellous, and believed that my little clay pitcher was enchanted. We used to leave it, filled to the brim, on the red-hot stove-plate, and at times, when all the water had seeped through the pores, the jar remained dry and unbroken; yet if a drop of water remained, this was always icy cold, even though the heat of the stove blackened any wood we may have placed on it.

This handsome jug, circled by a garland of ivy picked from the outer wall, would have pleased the eyes of artists more than gilding of our modern Sèvres porcelain. The Pleyel piano, wrested from the hands of the customs officials after three weeks of negotiation and four hundred francs in dues, filled the lofty, echoing vault of the cell with a glorious sound. Finally, the sacristan had consented to move into our cell a large and splendid Gothic chair of carved oak, which was being eaten away by worms and rats in an ancient Carthusian chapel. The frame served us as a book-case, while, by the light of our lamps, its pierced fretwork and tapering spires cast rich lacy shadows with magnificent pinnacles on the wall, restoring the ancient monastic character of the cell.

Our ex-landlord, Señor Gómez, the wealthy individual who had secretly let *Son Vent* to us, for it is not respectable for a Majorcan to speculate with his property, made a great scene and threatened legal action because we had damaged a few earthenware plates, for which he made us pay as though they had been Chinese porcelain. With more threats, he made us pay for the whitewashing and redecoration of the entire house, to disinfect it after our invalid's contagious cold. However, it is an ill wind that blows nobody any good, and in his anxiety to be rid of anything we had touched, he was eager to sell us all the household linen, and after much haggling, he insisted that we paid for the old linen at the prices of the new. So, thanks to him, we were not forced to sow flax in the hope of getting some sheets and tablecloths, like the Italian nobleman who had promised shirts to his pages.

You must not accuse me of childishness when I describe my annoyances which have left me with no deeper resentment than a lighter purse; yet no one can deny that the most interesting subject of study in any foreign country is most certainly the people. When I say that in all my financial dealings with the Majorcans, no matter how trivial, I met only with shameless dishonesty and gross greed; and when I add that they paraded their religious devotion before us by pretending to be shocked at our lack of faith, one will agree that the piety of simple souls, now so highly extolled by certain Conservatives, is not always the most edifying and moral of phenomenona, and we should be allowed, if we so desire, to have a different way of understanding and worshipping God. Yes, I have heard all the same stock phrases repeated over and over again: that it is criminal and dangerous to undermine even a misguided or corrupt faith, for there is nothing with which to replace it; that those, uncontaminated by the poison of philosophical investigation and revolutionary hysteria, are the only moral, hospitable and sincere people; that they still have poetry, greatness and the ancient virtues, etc., etc., ... And, I must confess, that here in Majorca, these solemn arguments made me laugh more than anywhere else. And when I saw my children, brought up in that abomination of desolation, Philosophy, gladly serving and attending a sick friend by themselves, while a hundred and sixty thousand Majorcans would have turned away, with a cruel lack of feeling and the most abject terror of an illness that was supposed to be contagious, I told myself that there was more courage and charity in my little scoundrels than in that whole population of saints and apostles.

These pious servants of God did not fail to accuse me of a great crime in exposing my children to the infection, and prophesied that Heaven, to punish my blindness, would strike them down with the same disease. I replied that, in our family, if one of us had the plague, the others would stay by his bedside, for it was not the custom in France, neither before the Revolution nor after, to desert the sick; that during the Napoleonic Wars, Spanish prisoners suffering from the most frightful diseases, were cared for by our peasants who, after sharing a bowl of soup and their clothing, had made over their beds to them and nursed them; that many had fallen victims to such charity and died of the infection, but that this did not prevent the survivors from continuing their hospitable and charitable works. The Majorcans just shook their heads with pitying smiles. The idea of selfless service to a stranger could not enter their heads, for it was as incomprehensible as that of behaving honestly or even obligingly to a foreigner.

All travellers who have visited the interior of the island wonder at the disinterested hospitality shown by the Majorcan farmer. They write admiringly, that despite the lack of inns in the country, it is none the less easy and most pleasant to tour, for a *simple letter of introduction* would be enough to be received, lodged and entertained free of charge. As I see it, this letter of introduction is not quite so simple as might appear. These travellers have omitted to mention that all classes in Majorca, that is to say all the inhabitants, are linked by a community of interests which establishes friendly relations among themselves, but in which neither religious charity nor human feeling plays any part. A few words will explain the pecuniary circumstances.

The aristocracy is rich in capital, poor in income, and ruined by the loans they have been obliged to raise. The many Jews, who are rich in ready money, hold all the *Cavallers'* lands in their wallets, and are, one can say, the real owners of the island; thus the *Cavallers* are no more than noble representatives commissioned to do the honours of their domains and palaces, one for the other, as well as for the occasional foreigners who visit the island. To fulfil this demanding task in proper style, they have to annually borrow from the Jews, and each year the snowball gets bigger. Earlier on I explained how land revenues are paralysed due to the lack of openings for industry; but there is a point of honour among the indigent *Cavallers*, which is to achieve ruin in their own good time, without abandoning luxury, or rather the spendthrift and extravagant ways of their forefathers.

The interests of the money-lenders are therefore closely linked to those of the farmers, a part of whose rent they collect by virtue of the title-deeds made over to them by the *Cavallers*.

Thus the *pagès*, who perhaps gains by this division of his debts, pays as little as possible to his landlord, and as much as possible to the banker. The lord is helpless and dependent, the Jew relentless and patient. He makes concessions, affects great tolerance, he gives time, but pursues his aim with diabolical genius: once he has his clutches on a property, before long, it must all come to him; his interest is to prove crucial until the debt reaches the value of the security. In twenty years time there will be no stately home left in Marjorca. The Jews will hold power, as is in France, and will raise their heads, which now are bowed in hypocritical servility beneath an ill-disguised disdain of the nobility and a puerile hatred of the common people. In the meantime, they are the true landowners, and the *pagès* fears them. He turns sadly to his old master; and tenderly crying, he wrests the largest share he can from his remaining fortune. His concern lies in satisfying both these powers, and in humouring them as far as possible lest he be crushed between them.

So, arm yourself with an introduction to one of the *pagès*, whether from a nobleman or someone rich, (and from whom else could it be, since there is no middle-class in Majorca?), and at once, the peasants' door will be open to you. But try asking for a glass of water without the introduction, and you will see what happens!

Yet the Majorcan *pagès* is a gentle, kind creature with peaceful habits and a calm and patient nature. He has no love of evil and no knowledge of good. He goes to confession, he prays, and thinks incessantly of how to procure his entry to Paradise, yet is ignorant of the true responsibility of humanity. You can no more hate him than you could an ox or a sheep, for he is more a savage than a man. He recites his prayers, he is as superstitious as a heathen and would eat his fellow-man without remorse, were that the custom of his country, and were he unable to fill himself with pork. He cheats, extorts, lies, insults and plunders without scruple. A foreigner is not a fellow-man for him. He would never rob his neighbour of so much as an olive: for in God's great design of things, those human beings from across the sea exist only to bring small profits to the Majorcan.

We nick-named Majorca the "Island of Monkeys", because, when surrounded by these cunning, thieving and yet innocent creatures, we grew accustomed to protect ourselves from them, and felt no more rancour or scorn than what the Indians feel towards chimpanzees or mischievous, shy orang-utangs.

Nevertheless, you get used to the sight of these creatures, clothed in human form and stamped with the seal of God, vegetating in an aimless existence isolated from contemporary humanity. It is sad that these imperfect beings are endowed with powers of understanding and perfectibility, that their future is the same as those more advanced races, and that it is only a question of time, perhaps rather long for us, but imperceptible in the abyss of eternity, before they achieve it. But the more you sense this perfectibility, the more you suffer to see them chained to the past. Though you might be frightened and upset, Providence does not appear troubled by this break in time. You feel in your heart, your mind and the depth of your being, that the lives of all others are bound up with your own, that nobody can exist without loving or being loved, understanding or being understood, helping or being helped. A feeling of intellectual and moral superiority can only give pleasure to the proud. I imagine the great desire of all generous people is not to sink to the level of their inferiors, but, to raise them to their own level in the twinkling of an eye, where they could at last live the true life of sympathy, communication, equality and brotherhood, which is the religious ideal of the human conscience.

I am certain that this desire lies at the bottom of every heart, and those who fight it, believing they can stifle it with insincere argument, must feel a deep and bitter, nameless pain. The people at the bottom, wear themselves out and fade away because they are unable to rise; those at the top become angry and impatient, tired of vainly stretching out a helping hand; while those who have no wish to help, consumed with boredom and fears of loneliness, sink lower than the lowest, into a bestial existence.

Chapter IV

S O we were alone in Majorca, as alone as if we had been living in a desert; and once our battle with the *monkeys* had been done and our daily bread won, we sat around the stove and made fun of it all. But as the winter advanced, the gloom froze all my attempts at gaiety and calm. Our invalid's state of health grew steadily worse; the wind howled in the ravine, the rain beat on our windows, the thunder sounded through our thick walls, mingling its mournful sound with the children's laughter and games. The eagles and vultures, emboldened by the mist, swooped down and snatched our poor sparrows from the pomegranate-tree which blocked my window. All boats were kept in port by a furious sea; we felt like prisoners, far from any enlightened help or productive sympathy. Death seemed to hover over our heads, waiting to seize one of us, while we alone battled to ward it off its prey. There was no human being around us who did not wish to hasten him to his grave and so put an end to the supposed danger of his proximity. This hostile thought became horribly depressing; but in ourselves we felt strong enough to replace the help and sympathy we were denied with care and sacrifice. I believe that at such times of trial the heart expands, and affection is heightened and fortified by the great strength it draws from a feeling of human solidarity. So we were deeply distressed to find ourselves cast among beings who did not understand this, and who, far from showing any sympathy, became objects of our deepest pity.

In addition I was baffled by a number of problems. I had no scientific knowledge whatsoever, and I would have had to be a doctor, and a very good one at that, in order to treat this illness responsibly, and this weighed heavily on my heart.

The doctor who visited us, whose skill and talent I do not doubt, had made a mistake, as any doctor may, even the most famous; every sincere practitioner will admit that he has often done so. The bronchitis had now been succeeded by a nervous condition which produced some of the symptoms of laryngeal phthisis.

At certain moments the doctor had observed these symptoms, but he had not seen the contrary symptoms which I witnessed at other times, and therefore prescribed a treatment suitable for consumptives: namely bleeding, starvation and a milk diet. We believed all this to be a great mistake, and that the bleeding would prove fatal. The invalid himself knew it instinctively, and so did I, for I had the same foreboding, having nursed many sick people and even though I knew nothing of medicine. I was terrified that my instinct might let me down, and I was fearful of opposing a learned man; so that when I saw the illness gaining ground, I was filled with great anxiety, as everyone will understand. "A bleeding will save him," I was told, "If you refuse it, he will die." But I was assured, even in my sleep, by a voice deep inside of me: "A bleeding will kill him, and if you prevent it , he will live." I am convinced that this was the voice of Providence, and today our friend, the terror of Majorca, has been declared no more consumptive than I am, and I thank Heaven for not allowing me to loose that confidence which saved us.

The diet did not agree with him. When we saw the ill effects, we kept to it as little as possible, but unfortunately the only option we had was to recur to either the local strongly spiced foods or hold a very frugal table. Milk products, the harmful effects of which we came to notice later, were very scarce in Majorca and so did him little harm. At that time we still thought that milk would work wonders, and took great pains to procure a supply. There are no cows on those mountains, and although the goat's milk we bought was always sampled by the children who delivered it, the jug never failed to arrive full. This miracle was performed every morning by the pious messenger, who always stopped in the courtyard by the Charterhouse well to say his prayers. To put an end to these marvels, we acquired a goat. She was the most gentle and friendly creature in the world, a lovely little African nanny, with short chamois-coloured hair, a hornless head, a blunt nose and drooping ears. These animals differ greatly from ours. They have the same cervine coat and ovine profile, but lack the frolicsome, mischievous air of our playful kids. On the contrary, they seem full of melancholy. They also differ from ours in having small udders that produce very little milk. When fully grown their milk has a wild, tangy flavour greatly loved by the Majorcans, but most offensive to us.

Our new little friend in the Charterhouse was enjoying her first maternity; she was hardly two years old, and her milk had a fine, delicate taste; but she was very stingy, especially when, parted from the herd she had been accustomed to - no, not to gambol (she was too serious, too Majorcan for that), but to wander on the mountain tops, she fell into a deep depression, which in many ways was similar to our own. Many fine weeds still flourished in the courtyard, and, in our small garden, aromatic plants, planted not so long ago by the Carthusians: but nothing could reconcile her to captivity. Bleating mournfully, she would wander, lost and disconsolate, through the cloisters. We bought a fat sheep to keep her company; a sheep, with thick white fleece six inches long, like those we see at home only in toyshop windows or on our grandmother's fans. This fine companion did a lot to restore the goat's tranquillity, and she now gave us some fairly creamy milk. But, although well fed, they both produced such a small quantity of milk, that we began to suspect the frequent visits paid by Maria Antonia, Catalina and the Niña to our livestock. We therefore locked them into a small yard at the foot of the church-tower and milked them ourselves. Mixing this very light milk with the milk of almonds, which my children and I took turns in expressing, resulted in a fairly wholesome and pleasant infusion. There was not much else we could use. All the drugs obtainable in Palma were intolerably dirty. The badly refined sugar imported from the mainland was oily and black, with a purgative effect on those unaccustomed to it.

One day we thought we had been saved, for we saw some violets growing in a wealthy farmer's garden. He permitted us to pick some for an infusion, and once we had gathered our little bunch, he charged us at the rate of one sou per violet: one Majorcan sou being the equivalent of three French ones.

In addition to these domestic cares, we had to sweep our rooms and make the beds ourselves if we wanted to sleep at night; because the Majorcan maid could not touch them without leaving us, with great generosity on her part, the same creatures my children had been amused to observe on the back of a roast chicken. Very few hours were left for work and walks; but they were well employed. The children worked well at their lessons, after which we could leave our miserable cell and enter into the most diverse and exquisite landscape. Each step, within that vast frame-work of mountains, offered some picturesque scene: a small chapel perched on a sheer rock, a thicket of rhododendrons almost falling down a rugged slope, a hermitage set beside a spring filled with tall reeds, a clump of trees growing among huge, ivy-covered boulders. When the sun deigned to appear for a moment, all these plants, all these stones and all these rainwashed lands, sparkled with some incredibly brilliant and fresh colours.

We had two particularly interesting walks. Despite the perfect views, I have no pleasant memories of the first, because our invalid, who was in good health at the time (it was at the beginning of our stay in Majorca) wanted to come with us; and the resultant exhaustion was to be the commencement of his illness.

Our goal was a hermitage situated on the sea-coast, some three miles from the Charterhouse. We followed the right arm of the mountain range, climbing from hill to hill along a stony path which cut our feet, until we reached the northern coast. At each turn of the path, through beautiful vegetation, we had magnificent views of the sea stretched out far below us. It was the first time that I saw fertile shores, covered with trees and shrubs down to the first wave, with no bare cliffs, desolate dunes or muddy beaches. In all the parts of the French coast that I know, even from the heights of Port-Vendres where I at last could experience its full beauty, I have always found the sea dirty and unpleasant to approach. The Lido, the pride of Venice, has horribly bare stretches of sand, inhabited by thousands of huge lizards that dart out from under your feet and start chasing you in ever increasing number, as in a nightmare. In Royant, near Marseilles, and I believe on almost all our coasts, a belt of sticky seaweed and sterile sand spoils the approach to the sea. In Majorca I was finally able to see the sea of my dreams, transparent and as blue as the sky, a sapphire plain carefully ploughed into gently undulating furrows which, if you are looking down from a certain height, seems unmoving and framed by dark green forests. Each step we took on the mountain offered us a new view, each more magnificent than the last. We had a long climb down before reaching the hermitage. Yet this very lovely part of the coast did not have that majestic quality which I found at another part of the coast some months later.

There was nothing poetic about the four or five hermits living there. Their dwelling was as wretched and miserable as their profession demanded, and their terraced garden, which they were digging when we arrived, overlooked a vast and lonely expanse of sea stretching out before their eyes. We found them to be the most stupid people in the world. They wore no religious habit. The superior left his spade and came to us, wearing

The Hermitage, at the present time.

a shapeless, beige jacket; there was nothing picturesque about his short hair and dirty beard. He spoke of the hard life he had, and of the unbearable cold on this part of the coast; but when we asked him whether they ever had frost, we were unable to make him understand what frost was. He did not know the word in any language, and had never heard of any countries colder than Majorca. Nevertheless, he had some idea of France for he had seen, in 1830, our fleet sail past on its way to capture Algiers; this had been the finest, the most amazing, and one might say only, sight of his life. He asked us if the French had indeed conquered Algiers; and when we told him that they had recently also taken Constantine, his eyes opened wide and he exclaimed that the French were a great nation.

He then led us to a very dirty little cell, and introduced us to the senior hermit. We took him for a centenarian, and were surprised to learn that he was only eighty. He looked a complete imbecile, automatically carving wooden spoons with his shaky, dirty hands. He paid no attention to us although he was not deaf; but when the superior addressed him, he raised his huge head which resembled a wax-work, and showed us his witless face. A lifetime of intellectual degradation marked his drawn face, and I hastily averted eyes from one of the most horrifying and painful sights I had ever witnessed. We gave them alms because they belong to a mendicant Order, and enjoy great veneration among the peasants, who see they lack nothing.

Returning to Palma by way of the Charterhouse, a violent wind arose and blew us over several times, which made our progress tiring and exhausted our invalid.

The second walk took place a few days before our departure from Majorca, and left such an impression on me that I shall never forget it as long as I live. Never had such scenic splendour gripped me more, and I doubt whether I have been equally affected more than three or four times in my life.

The rains had at last ceased, and Spring was suddenly there. It was now February, with all the almond trees in bloom and the

The Hermitage of Valldemossa. The terraced garden.

fields filled with fragrant jonquils. This was, apart from the colour of the sky and the vibrant tones of the landscape, the only difference one noted between the two seasons; for most of the trees are evergreen. Those which send up early shoots are never caught by frost; the grass stays green, and the flowers need only one morning of sunshine to show their faces to the wind. Even when our little garden lay half a foot under snow, lovely little climbing roses were swayed by a gust of wind on our trellises. Though somewhat pale, they looked quite happy.

Often, from the northern door of the monastery, I used to gaze at the sea, and finally, when our invalid was well enough to be left alone for two or three hours, my children and I set out to explore that stretch of coast. Until then I had not felt the least curiosity in seeing it, but my children who ran like the chamois, had assured me that it was the most beautiful place in the world. Whether our visit to the hermitage, the original cause of all this sorrow, had left me with a deep-seated resentment, or perhaps after having seen such beautiful views of the sea from the mountains, I did not expect the view from sea level to equal it, and had not been tempted to leave the sheltered valley of Valldemossa.

As I have already explained, the Charterhouse stands on a gentle, north-sloping plain at a the point where the mountain range divides into two broad-spreading arms. Gazing daily at the sea rising to the horizon from far below this plain, my eyes and my judgement had made a grave error. Instead of realizing that the plain, after first rising, suddenly dropped away, I assumed that that it sloped gently down to the sea-shore some five or six leagues away. Yet, how was I to know that the sea, which seemed to be level with the Charterhouse, actually lay two or three thousand feet below us? Being so far away, I was at times amazed at its loud roar, and failed to account for this phenomenon. I do not understand why I allow myself to mock the Parisian bourgeoisie when my own conclusions can be, at times, so foolish? I had not realized that the horizon which I used to

The Magnificent Coastline, as seen from the Mirador of the Hermitage.

gaze upon, was fifteen or twenty leagues from the coast, whereas the waves broke on the shore of island a bare half hours walk by road from the Charterhouse. So when my children used to urge me to come and look at the sea, saying it was only a few steps away, I never found the time, thinking that what seemed only a few children's steps were, in fact, a few giant's steps; for we all know that children walk with their heads, never thinking of their feet, and that the myth of Tom Thumb's seven-league boots is there to signify that children can circle the world without noticing that they have done it.

In the end I let them have their way, convinced that we would never reach that imaginary shore, which I believed to be so distant. My son claimed to know the way; but all ways are easy when you are wearing seven-league boots, and for sometime now I had been walking through life wearing only a pair of slippers, so I protested that, unlike him and his sister, I was unable to negotiate ditches, hedges and torrents. After a quarter of an hour I noticed that we were not descending toward the sea, for the rivulets were running swiftly towards us, and the farther we went, the farther the sea seemed to recede and the horizon sink. I was convinced he was mistaken, and decided to ask the first peasant I met, how to find our way down to the coast.

Under a clump of willows, in a muddy ditch, three shepherdesses, perhaps three fairies in disguise, were shovelling mud with their spades in search of some talisman or some salad. The first had only one tooth, and could have been the Fairy Dentue, who stirs evil spells into her stews with that horrible tooth. The second hag was, judging by her appearance, the evil hunchback Carabosse, the mortal foe of orthopaedic institutions. Both grimaced hideously at us. The first, clicking her tooth, approached my daughter, whose youth had awoken her appetite. The second, shook her head and brandished her crutch, as if wanting to hit my son's kidneys, for his slim, upright figure seemed to horrify her. But the third, who was young and pretty, jumped deftly to the edge of the ditch and, throwing her cloak over her shoulders, walked off gesturing us to follow. She was certainly a good little fairy; but in her mountain disguise liked to call herself *Périca de Pier-Bruno*.

Périca is the nicest Majorcan I ever met. She and my goat are the only creatures in Valldemossa who have a small corner of my heart. The little girl was so coated in mud that she would have made my goat blush; but after having walked a short distance through the damp grass, her bare feet reappeared, not exactly white, but as dainty as those of an Andalusian girl, and her lovely smile, her confiding and curious chatter, her unselfish readiness to help, made us feel we had found a priceless pearl. She was sixteen years old, with delicate features; a round velvety face like a peach; she had the line and beauty of a greek statue; a reed-slender waist and tanned, naked arms. From beneath a coarse linen *rebozillo* her hair flowed, loose and tangled, like a filly's tail. She led us to the end of the field, then across a meadow strewn with boulders and edged with trees; by now the sea had completely dissapeared, and we were once again climbing the mountain, and I had the feeling that Périca was playing with us.

She suddenly opened a little gate at the end of a field, and we saw a path that wound its way about a huge sugar-loaf rock. We followed its turnings and, as if by magic, found ourselves above the sea, overlooking its vastness, with the coast lying a league below our feet. This unexpected view left me quite dizzy and my first reaction was to sit down. Slowly but surely I conquered my fear and plucked up some courage to follow the path, which was more suitable for goats than human beings. What I saw was so beautiful that for once I had swallow-wings in my head, and not seven-league boots; I set off between the tall limestone needles which rose like giants, fifty to eighty feet high, along the the crest of the cliff, trying to see the bottom of a small cove that had formed a deep hollow on my right hand, where the fishermen's boats seemed hardly bigger than flies.

Suddenly I saw nothing before or below me but the pure

blue sea. The path had gone off on its own, I am not sure where; Périca was shouting from somewhere above my head and my children, who were following me on all fours, began to shout even more loudly. Turning, I saw my daughter in tears; so I retraced my steps to find out what was wrong; and, after a moment's thought, I realized that there was good reason for the childrens' fear and despair. One step more, and I should have descended far too rapidly, unless I had managed to walk upside down, like a fly on the ceiling, for those rocks onto which I had ventured, jutted out over the bay, and the base of the cliff was deeply eroded. When I saw the danger into which I had led my children, I was horribly frightened and hurriedly climbed back to them; but once I had placed them safely behind one of those giant sugar-loaves, I once again had the urge to look at the bottom of the cove and the underside of the cliff.

Never had I seen anything like what I had glimpsed there, and my imagination took wing. I descended by another path, clutching at brambles and hugging stone pinnacles, each of which marked a new drop. At last I was able to catch glimpses of the enormous hollow where the waves sounded with uncanny music. I do not know what magical harmonies I was hearing, nor what unknown world I had discovered, for I was suddenly pulled back by my frightened and very angry son. Most unromantically, I fell backwards into a rational sitting posture, and not forwards, which would have been the end of my adventure and me. The child then reproached me with such fervour that I abandoned my project, though not without a feeling of regret which still haunts me; for my slippers grow heavier every year, and I do not think that the wings I found that day will ever regrow and fly me to shores like those.

There is no doubt, of course, that what one sees does not always match with what one dreams, I know this as well as anyone else, but this only applies to the arts and the works of man. As far as I am concerned, and whether it is because I have a lazy and mediocre imagination, or whether God is more gift-ed than I (which is quite possible), I have more often found that Nature is infinitely more beautiful than I can anticipate; and I do not remember finding her sullen, unless I was in a sullen mood myself.

I shall never forgive myself for not having gone round that last rock. Might I not have seen Amphitrite herself, under a vault of mother-of-pearl, her brow crowned with whispering seaweeds? Instead, I saw only limestone pinnacles, rising from gorge to gorge like stalactites from cave to cave, each assuming some strange shape or bizarre posture. Hardy trees, deformed and half up-rooted by the winds, leaned over the abyss, and at the base of this abyss another mountain rose to meet the sky, a mountain of crystal, diamond and sapphire. The sea, as every one knows, viewed from a great height creates the illusion of being a vertical plane. Explain this, if you wish.

My children now insisted on collecting some plants. The most beautiful liliaceae in the world grow among these rocks. Between the three of us we finally managed to pull up a bulb of the crimson amaryllis, but we had to abandon it before reaching the Charterhouse because of its weight. My son cut this wonderful plant into pieces to show our invalid a fragment, the size of his head. Périca, carrying a large bundle of sticks which she had picked up on the way, with which, with her sudden and brusque movements, she constantly bumped us, led the way back to the outskirts of the village. I forced her to come with us to the Charterhouse to give her a small present, which I had great difficulty in persuading her to accept. Poor, sweet Périca! you neither had, nor ever will have, any idea of the good you did when you showed me that among the monkeys there was one sweet, gentle and helpful human being who had no ulterior motive. That evening we all rejoiced that we had met an understanding and caring individual before we left Valldemossa.

Chapter V

B ETWEEN these two walks, the first and the last in Majorca, we had taken several others which I shall not describe for the fear of boring the reader with my enthusiasm for the all-round beauty of Nature here, scattered with picturesque homes, each attempting to outdo the other, cottages, palaces, churches, monasteries. If one of our great landscape painters ever visits Majorca, I draw his attention to a country house named *La Granja de Fortuñy*, with its valley of citrus trees extending from its marble colonnades, including the entire road leading there. But, without having to go out that far, he need hardly take ten steps on that enchanted island before having to pause at every bend in the path, now before a Moorish reservoir shaded by palm-trees, now before a finely carved fifteenth century cross, now on the edge of an olive grove.

The forceful, yet bizarre shapes of these olive trees, these Majorcan foster-fathers, are unequalled. The islanders swear that no olive plantation is more recent than the time of the Romans. Even if I wished to, I cannot dispute this, for I have no way of proving the contrary. After one look at their daunting appearance, the incredible size and frenzied attitudes of these mysterious trees, my imagination voluntarily accepted them as contemporaries of Hannibal. In the evening, when walking in their shade you have to remind yourself that they are trees; for if you believe your imagination and what your eyes see, you would be terror-stricken by these fantastic monsters, some bending over towards you like enormous dragons, with gaping jaws and wings outspread; others coiled up on themselves like boa-constrictors; others, like giant wrestlers, locked together in furious combat. Here, a galloping centaur carrying a hideous monkey on his rump; there some nameless reptile devouring a panting doe; further on, a satyr dancing with a he-goat a little uglier than himself; and often, a single tree, split, gnarled, twisted and deformed, which you mistake for a group of ten different trees, passes off as all these different monsters and unites once again to form a single head, as horrible as an Indian fetish, crested with a single green branch. Anyone interested enough to glance at M. Lauren's engravings need not fear that he exaggerated the appearance of his olive-trees. He could have chosen even more extraordinary examples, and I hope that the *Magazine Pittoresque*, that amusing and un-tiring popularizer of the wonders of art and nature, will set out one fine morning to collect some first-class examples.

In order to convey the splendour of these sacred trees, from which one expects to hear the sound of prophetic voices, and the glittering sky against which their sharp silhouettes are drawn, nothing less than Rousseau's [27, 28] bold and impressive brushstrokes are needed. Limpid water where asphodels and myrtles are mirrored calls for Dupré.[29] The more formal and organized landscapes, where liberated nature adds a proud and classical air, would prove a great temptation for the severe Corot.[30] But to reproduce this confused mass of grasses, wild

---

[27] Pierre Étienne Théodore Rousseau, 1812-1867 *(Translator's note.)*

[28] Rousseau, one of the greatest landscape-painters of our day, hardly known to the public, thanks to the obstinacy of the juries who, for many years denied him the right to exhibit his masterpieces.

[29] Jules Dupré, 1811-1889, a well known landscape artist, and one of the leaders of the Barbizon group of landscape painters. *(Translator's note.)*

[30] Jean-Baptiste Camille Corot, 1796-1875, a great master of landscape painting, who inspired and to some extent anticipated the landscape paintings of the Impressionists. *(Translator's note.)*

flowers, ancient trunks, and garlands cascading over hidden fountains where storks wet their long legs, I would wish to have at my command, like a magic wand, Huet's burin in my pocket.

When I saw an old Majorcan Cavalier on the threshold of his dilapidated palace, how often did I think of Decamps,[31] that great master who raised caricature to the level of historical painting, and who was a genius in giving wit, gaiety, poetry, in one word, life, to bare walls? Those beautiful, sun-tanned children who played in our cloister, dressed up as monks, would have delighted him. He would have had crowds of monkeys there, and angels among them, pigs with human faces, grubby little cherubs among the pigs; Périca, lovely as Galatea, covered in mud, and laughing in the sunshine as if all on earth was sweet.

But it is you, Eugène,[32] my dear old friend, my dear artist, whom, one night, I should have liked to lead up the mountain flooded by moonlight.

It was in this lovely countryside that I was nearly drowned along with my poor fourteen year old son, yet he did not lack courage, any more than I lost the power of seeing how Nature that evening had become unsurpassingly romantic, unsurpassingly mad and altogether sublime.

My son and I had left Valldemossa, during the winter rains, to go and persuade the fierce customs officials in Palma to release the Pleyel piano. It had been a fairly clear morning, and the roads passable, but while we were in town it started to pour with rain again, worse than ever. Here, in France, we complain about the rain, but we do not know what it really means: the longest rainfall here last some two hours, where one storm-cloud follows another with always a short interval between the two. But in Majorca, a permanent cloud covers the island, and

---

[31] Alexandre Gabriel Descamps, 1803-1860. *(Translator's note.)*

[32] Eugène Ferdinand-Victor Delacroix, 1798-1863, a friend of the author. A great French painter, whose use of colour greatly influenced the development of both Impressionist and Post-impressionist painters. His inspiration came chiefly from historical or contemporary events. *(Translator's note.)*

The Charterhouse, a drawing by Maurice Sand.

remains there until it has rained itself dry; this could take forty or fifty hours, or as much as four or five days, without any break or lessening intensity.

Towards sunset we climbed back into the *birlocho*, hoping to reach the Charterhouse within three hours. It took us seven hours, and we almost slept with the frogs an the bottom of some unexpected lake. The coachman was in an awful temper; he found a thousand reasons for not setting out: his horse was un-shod, his mule was lame, the axle had broken, and I do not know what else! We now knew the Majorcans well enough not to believe him, and made him climb onto the cart, where for the first few hours he wore the most mournful of expressions. He did not sing, he refused our cigars, he did not even curse his mule, which was a very bad sign indeed; death seemed to have entered his soul. Hoping to frighten us, he had chosen the worst of the seven roads known to him. This road plunged lower and lower and we soon met the torrent, entered it and never left it. This admirable torrent, uncomfortable in its bed, had rolled out and inundated the road, turning it into a raging, roaring river which rushed rapidly towards us. When this spiteful coachman, who had counted on our fear, realized that we were determined to continue, he lost his temper and began to curse and swear loud enough to bring the heavens tumbling down about our ears. The hewn-stone channels which carry water from the spring to the city, were so swollen that they had burst like the frog in the fable; and then, having no where to go, it spread out and formed puddles, then pools, then lakes and finally an inland sea which flooded the whole countryside. Soon the coachman ran out of saints to vow to and devils to curse. He legs were soaked, which he well deserved, and found us not in the least bit inclined to be sorry for him. The carriage was water-tight, and we were still dry; but every moment, as my son said, 'the tide was rising'; we continued blindly, being knocked about horribly, and believing that each new pothole we fell into would become our grave. Finally we tilted so far over to one side that the mule stopped, as if to gather himself before breathing his last: the coachman dismounted and clambered up the bank of the road, which rose to the height of his head; but he stopped when, in the glimmering twilight, he saw that this was the bank of the Valdemossa canal which had become a river, and, at intervals, poured onto our path forming a river on a lower level.

It was a tragicomic moment. I had felt some fear for myself, and a great fear for my child. I looked at him; he was laughing at the coachman's face, who was standing straddled across the shafts, checking the abyss, without the least thought of being amused at our expense. When I saw my son so calm and cheerful, I regained my confidence in God. I felt he instinctively knew his fate, and I relied on that intuition which children are unable to put into words, but which diffuses their brow like a cloud or a ray of sunshine.

The coachman, seeing that there was no way of abandoning us to our fate, resigned himself to sharing it, and suddenly became heroic. 'Don't be afraid, my children,' he called in a fatherly voice; then uttering a great shout he lashed at his mule, which stumbled, fell, staggered up, fell again, and finally stumbled forward half drowned. The carriage leaned over, 'Get on!', then lurched to the other side, 'Get on, get on!' and with ominous creakings and prodigious leaps it emerged triumphant from its ordeal, like a ship which has scraped the rocks without splitting.

It seemed that we were saved, and we were dry; but it was necessary to restart this nautical journey by cart a dozen times before we reached the mountain. At last we reached the ramp; but the mule, exhausted and frightened by the sound of the torrent and the wind in the mountain, started backing towards the precipice. We climbed out and each pushed a wheel while the coachman pulled M. Aliboron by his long ears. We had do this innumerable times, and after two hours' climbing in which we had not advanced even half a league, and after the mule had come to a standstill on the bridge, trembling in every limb, we decided to leave man, carriage and beast there, and reach the Charterhouse on foot.

This proved no mean undertaking. The steep path had become a raging torrent which needed all the strength of our legs to battle against. Some smaller and unexpected torrents, gushing down noisily from the rocks above, would suddenly appear on our right, and we often had to make a dash to avoid them, or cross them with the thought that at any moment they could become impassable. The rain poured down; enormous clouds as black as ink covered the face of the moon; then, cloaked in greyish, impenetrable shadows, battered by an impetuous wind, feeling the tree-tops bend to brush our heads, hearing the sound of cracking firs and rolling stones, we were forced to stop and wait, as a poet once banteringly said, until Jupiter had relighted the snuffed candle.

It was during these intervals of shade and light, Eugène, that you would have seen, again and again, the most strange and sinister reflections and shadows as the sky and the earth paled and once again lit up. When the moon recovered her splendour, and wanted, it seemed, to rule a corner of deep blue that had been swiftly cleared for her by the wind, the dark clouds would reappear like phantoms keen to cloak her in the folds of their mantles. They over-ran her and would occasionally tear apart to reveal her as lovelier and more compassionate than ever. The mountain streaming with waterfalls, and the trees uprooted by the gale, suggested Chaos. We remembered that splendid witches' sabbath that you saw in some dream and which you sketched with some brush dipped in the red and blue waves of Phlegethon and Erebus. And barely had we gazed upon this hellish scene becoming real before our eyes, when the moon disappeared, devoured by monsters of the air, leaving us in bluish limbo, where we ourselves, like clouds, seemed to float, unable to see the ground on which we risked our feet.

Leaving the waters behind us, we at last reached the paved path of the last mountain, and were out of danger. We were overwhelmed with fatigue and barefooted, or nearly so; it had taken us three hours to cover the last league.

But the good weather returned and the Majorcan steamer was able resume its weekly journeys to Barcelona. Our invalid did not seem fit enough to stand the crossing, but neither was he fit enough to stand another week in Majorca. It was a frightening situation; there were days when I lost all hope and courage. To console us, Maria Antonia and her village cronies, served us with the most edifying conversations on future life. 'That consumptive,' they used to say, 'will go straight to Hell, first for being a consumptive, and secondly for never going to confession.' 'Of course, when he is dead, we will not bury him in consecrated ground, and as no one is prepared to bury him, his friends must manage best they can. How they will solve that problem, I don't know. I want to have nothing to do with it myself.' 'Nor I!' 'Nor I: and amen!'

At last we left, but I have already described the company and the hospitality we met on that Majorcan ship.

On reaching Barcelona, I was so pressed to end that eternity with that inhuman race, that I did not have the patience to wait for the formalities of disembarkation. I wrote a note to the naval commander, M. Belvès, and sent it to him by boat. Almost at once he came to fetch us in a small open boat and took to his ship, the *Meleager*.

Setting foot on this fine brig, as clean and elegant as a drawing room, we found ourselves surrounded by intelligent, pleasant faces, receiving generous and assiduous attention from the commander, the doctor, the officers and the crew; shaking hands with the delightful and witty French Consul, M. Gautier d'Arc, we jumped for joy on the bridge and cried from the bottom of our hearts: *'Vive la France!'* We felt we had come back from a world tour, and had left the Polynesian savages for the civilized world.

Now the moral of this story, childish perhaps, but sincere, is that man is not made to live with trees, stones, the clear sky, the blue sea, with the mountains and the flowers, but with his fellow-men.

During the stormy days of youth, we imagine that solitude is the sure refuge from peril, and a sure remedy for wounds of battle. This is a grave error, and experience teaches us that if we cannot live in peace with our fellow-men, neither poetic admiration nor aesthetic enjoyment will ever fill the gaping abyss at the bottom of our souls.

I have often dreamed of living in a desert, and every honest man will confess he has done the same. But believe me, my friends, we are too affectionate to live alone, and our only alternative is to live in mutual tolerance; for we are like children of the same womb, who may tease, squabble and even fight, but who can never part.

The End

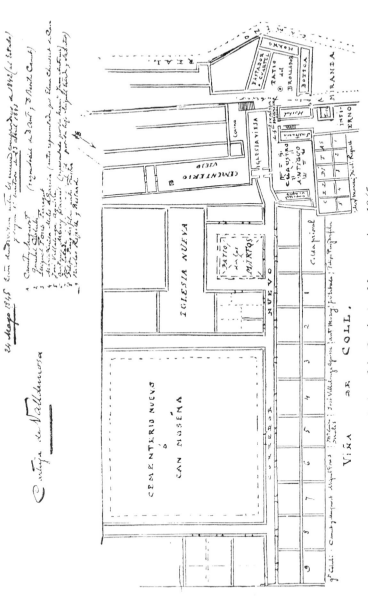

A plan of the Carthusian Monastery in 1845.